LITURGY FOR A N

C000077021

Also published by SPCK

TOWARDS LITURGY 2000

Preparing for the revision of
the Alternative Service Book

Paul Bradshaw   Mark Dalby   Martin Dudley
John Fenwick   Donald Gray   Derek Pattinson
Michael Perham   Bryan Spinks   Kenneth Stevenson

Edited by Michael Perham

LITURGY FOR A NEW CENTURY

FURTHER ESSAYS
IN PREPARATION FOR THE REVISION OF THE
ALTERNATIVE SERVICE BOOK

Martin Dudley   John Fenwick   Donald Gray

Michael Perham   Paul Roberts   Mark Santer

Bryan Spinks   David Stancliffe   Kenneth Stevenson

Edited by
Michael Perham

SPCK/Alcuin Club

First published in Great Britain 1991
for the Alcuin Club by

SPCK
Holy Trinity Church
Marylebone Road
London NW1 4DU

© The Alcuin Club 1991

All rights reserved. No part of this book may be reproduced or
transmitted in any form or by any means, electronic or
mechanical, including photocopying, recording, or by any
information storage and retrieval system, without permission in
writing from the publisher.

British Library Cataloguing in Publication Data

Liturgy for a new century.
1. Christian church. Public worship. Liturgical aspects
I. Dudley, Martin   II. Perham, Michael 1947–
264

ISBN 0-281-04499-6

Filmset by Pioneer Associates
Printed in Great Britain by
Whitstable Litho, Whitstable, Kent

ALCUIN CLUB COLLECTIONS No. 70

The Alcuin Club exists to promote the study of Christian liturgy in general, and in particular the liturgies of the Anglican Communion. Since its foundation in 1897 it has published over 130 books and pamphlets. Members of the Club receive some publications of the current year free and others at a reduced rate.

Information concerning the annual subscription, applications for membership and lists of publications is obtainable from the Treasurer, The Revd T. R. Barker, All Saints' Vicarage, Highlands Road, Runcorn, Cheshire WA7 4PS (Tel. 0928-575 666).

President

The Right Reverend E. W. Kemp, DD, Bishop of Chichester

Committee

The Reverend Canon D. C. Gray, MPhil, PhD, AKC, FRHistS, *Chairman*
The Reverend T. R. Barker, MA, *Treasurer*
The Reverend J. M. M. Dalby, MA, PhD
The Reverend M. R. Dudley, BD, MTh, AKC, DPS
The Reverend J. R. K. Fenwick, BSc, BA, MTh, STh, PhD
Sir Derek Pattinson, MA
The Reverend M. F. Perham, MA, *Secretary*
The Reverend P. J. Roberts, BA
The Reverend B. D. Spinks, BA, MTh, BD, DD, FRHistS
The Reverend K. W. Stevenson, MA, PhD, DD

Contents

CONTENTS

The Contributors

Martin Dudley is Vicar of Owlsmoor in Berkshire, and teaches Doctrine at Chichester Theological College.

John Fenwick is the Archbishop of Canterbury's Assistant Secretary for Ecumenical Affairs.

Donald Gray is a Canon of Westminster, Rector of St Margaret's, Westminster, and Speaker's Chaplain. He is Chairman of the Joint Liturgical Group and of the Alcuin Club.

Michael Perham is Rector of The Oakdale Team Ministry in Poole. He is a member of the Liturgical Commission, of the Archbishops' Commission on Church Music and of the General Synod. He is Chairman of Praxis.

Paul Roberts teaches Liturgy at Trinity College, Bristol.

Mark Santer is Bishop of Birmingham and Co-Chairman of the Anglican–Roman Catholic International Commission.

Bryan Spinks is Chaplain of Churchill College, Cambridge, and lectures in liturgy in the University of Cambridge. He is a member of the Liturgical Commission.

David Stancliffe is Provost of Portsmouth. He is a member of the Liturgical Commission, of the Council for the Care of Churches, and of the General Synod.

Kenneth Stevenson is Rector of Holy Trinity and St Mary's, Guildford, and a member of the Liturgical Commission. He is also Chairman of the Society of Liturgists and Secretary to the Anglo-Scandinavian Theological Conferences.

Preface

Liturgy for a New Century is a sequel to *Towards Liturgy 2000*, published by SPCK in July 1989. That first volume of essays began a process, which the Church of England has seemed eager to take up, of reflecting on a decade of use of *The Alternative Service Book 1980* with a view to finding the right sort of service book to take its place at the turn of the century. *Towards Liturgy 2000* was well received, and has helped to initiate a debate that must soon enable the Church to spell out the principles on which the new service book will be based, so that those charged with the detailed work, work that needs to be both creative and painstaking, may settle down quietly to their task, while the rest of the Church goes on with its worshipping, preaching and living through the liturgy it already has.

Liturgy for a New Century is not only a sequel, but also a response. Its authors have tried to listen to the emerging debate, and so have identified some new areas and particular services where people are seeking enrichment. In this series of essays, alongside the particular — eucharistic prayers, for instance — we have explored wider issues that will affect every section of a service book — ecumenism and evangelism, for instance.

There will be those who will be fearful that another decade, that ought to have quite other priorities, will be taken up with liturgical change that will confuse and even anger Christian people who are only now growing used to the 1980 revision and discovering its rich spiritual resources. But they can be

xi

reassured by these two volumes of essays. For whereas in the 1970s the major change was in the form of worship people encountered most and that goes deepest with them, the Eucharist, that service is the one that in the 1990s can be left almost unaltered in its basic structures and texts. Enrichment there can be, but there need not and should not be the dramatic changes that Series 2 Holy Communion brought to the structure and Series 3 to the language of the rite. The 1990s need not see liturgy dividing the Church. Indeed the 2000 service book ought to be one that brings some healing to a Church where worship has brought some hurt, as well as joyful freshness, in the last generation.

Back in the 1920s, the Alcuin Club, with its reputation for sound English liturgical scholarship, took a leading part in the liturgical debate in that abortive round of prayer book revision. Now, at the beginning of the 1990s, once again the Alcuin Club is trying to play a constructive and thought-provoking role in stimulating liturgical discussion in the Church. The Club is grateful to Kenneth Stevenson for first suggesting the titles and authors of these essays. Once again we have been able to draw in the main on the liturgical expertise that exists within the Club's committee for the essays in this book, though we record our thanks also to Mark Santer and David Stancliffe for responding to the invitation to join us in this venture.

Everyone will have their favourite chapter in a book like this, and probably also the one with which they least agree. It is not the task of the editor to suggest where the reader may find the most compelling argument. But perhaps it ought to be said that Mark Santer's 'The Praises of God' is a crucial starting point to which all the contributors would subscribe, because, for all our concern for detail and for texts, our real passion as liturgists is for the worship of God, for words and rituals that deepen our relationship with him, and for liturgy that can lift us to Heaven. And Bryan Spinks's postscript on the resourcing of liturgy is crucial too, for liturgy on the cheap will never enable the Church to worship God well.

Michael Perham
May 1990

1

The Praises of God

MARK SANTER

Ask people why they go to a particular church, or why they stay away. Part of the answer, if not all of it, will have to do with worship. They like it high, they like it low, they like it free, they like it formal. Their answers may be good or bad in the judgement of the professionals. Nevertheless the instinct is sound. People are right in thinking that the quality and manner of worship are central. They do not have to come to church; and if they come, they want to worship God in ways they find possible and edifying.

There is of course more to being a Christian than going to church. Worship is dead if it is cut off from daily life. But this perception is abused if it leads to the devaluing of the activity of worship as somehow peripheral to such matters as the confession and practice of the faith, or if the theology and study of liturgy are neglected as less deserving of serious intellectual attention than the study of the Bible, doctrine or ethics.

Worship is in fact central to the corporate life of the Church. It is above all in assembling together for prayer that we identify ourselves as believers, and this in two ways. Internally, we identify ourselves as belonging to each other; externally, as distinct from those who do not pray with us. It is in meeting for worship that the Church is made visible as a public and corporate entity. Concern for worship is therefore inseparable from concern for mission and evangelization. It is no accident that worship has so often been the focus of persecution.

It is worship, either in the home or in church, that sustains the life of the Christian community when everything else is taken away. For more than seventy years the Christians of the Soviet Union have lived without schools, social work and catechization. Priests have been unable to minister to people in their homes. The Lord has kept his Church alive by the prayers taught by grandmothers to their grandchildren, and by the Church's public liturgy.

Only when worship becomes detached from reality, either from the realities of the world or from the reality of God, does it become an irrelevance. When that happens, it is a sign that faith itself is in peril.

Discussions of liturgy turn quickly to practicalities — to matters of language, rite, ceremonial and setting. But the practicalities of what is said and done always imply some kind of a theory, some kind of an understanding of what it is all about, even if we have not thought about it very clearly. Sometimes we need to stand back and think about first principles. If we can get the theology straight, it will help us to discern and order our practical priorities.

Scripture teaches us that creation has its beginning and end in the worship of God. 'Where were you', says the Lord to Job, 'when I laid the foundation of the earth . . ., when the morning stars sang together, and all the sons of God shouted for joy?' (Job 38.4, 7). As James Montgomery put it:

> Songs of praise the angels sang,
> Heaven with alleluias rang,
> When creation was begun,
> When God spake and it was done.

And at the end:

> Heaven and earth must pass away,
> Songs of praise shall crown that day,
> God will make new heavens and earth,
> Songs of praise shall hail their birth.

Montgomery is echoing both the Book of Job and the songs heard by St John the Divine: 'The voice of a great multitude, like the sound of many waters and like the sound of mighty thunderpeals, crying, "Hallelujah! For the Lord our God the Almighty reigns. Let us rejoice and exult and give him the glory"' (Rev. 19.6–7).

From beginning to end creation is enfolded in the praises of heaven. The praises are heard on earth as well as in heaven: in heaven when the angels sing before the throne of God; on earth when humans join with angels and archangels and all the hosts of heaven in praising God and saying, 'Holy, holy, holy is the Lord God of hosts! Heaven and earth are full of his glory!'

When the end comes, when there is a new heaven and a new earth, and the city of God comes down to earth, and there is no more veil between earth and heaven, and all is on earth as it is in heaven; then, we are told, there will be no temple to mediate God's presence to humanity. God will be his own temple, and the servants of God will see him face to face. He will be all, and in all, immediately present to his people.

But the end has not yet come. Christ's work indeed is done, he is risen from the dead, he has returned to his Father, the way from earth to heaven is open. But we are still on earth. Our risen life is still *hidden* with Christ in God. We see indeed, but only in a glass darkly, not yet face to face. We are still in the days of our pilgrimage.

So although we repeat the words of the psalm, 'I will bless the Lord at all times', we say them in hope. We know that we cannot in fact bless God at *all* times. The best we can do is to bless him at particular times. We cannot worship him everywhere; we have to worship him somewhere. So God gives us sacraments, as particular signs of his universal grace. His glory fills all heaven and earth; but he gives us temples where his glory may be found. The risen Christ is everywhere present; but he makes himself findable where two or three meet together in his name. His sacrifice, offered once for all, the sacrifice that removes the veil between earth and heaven — it stands for ever, never to be repeated. But we need to be put in mind of it again and again, not just in general but in particular. So week by week and day by day, in the temples and at the altars which God appoints, the Holy Spirit makes the Lord's sacrifice present to us, so that we may share in its fruits in the only place and at the only time that we can, which is here and now.

God gives us sacraments — not just baptism and the Eucharist, but the whole sacramental order — so that, while still on earth, we may have windows into heaven. We meet together in the name of the Lord so as to lose ourselves and find ourselves again as children of God. We come together now in the assembly of the Lord to receive a pledge and foretaste of what we are promised in the end: heaven and earth made new, with heaven brought down to earth and earth taken up into heaven.

We meet to praise God, not because he needs our prayers and praises, but because we need to offer them. In offering our prayer and our praise, we realize what we are and what we shall be, God's own children, redeemed and recreated in the image of his Son. When we meet in the name of the Lord, he stands in our midst, we hear his Word, no mere voice from the past but living and active, and the Holy Spirit assures us that God's promises are a reality — such as the promise heard by St John: 'Behold, the dwelling of God is with men. He will dwell with them, and they shall be his people, and God himself will be with them; he will wipe away every tear from their eyes, and death shall be no more, neither shall there be mourning nor crying nor pain any more, for the former things have passed away' (Rev. 21.3-4).

Through the sacramental order, Christ, risen from the dead and seated at the Father's right hand in heaven, mediates to us who are still on earth the fruits of his sacrifice. Christ the High Priest of God's new and eternal covenant has, by his self-offering completed on the cross, broken down once for all the divide between heaven and earth, not for his own sake but for ours, so that united with him we too may enter the Holy of Holies and see God face to face. He gave himself for us, so that through him, with him and in him we may be able to offer our own lives to God — and not our own lives only, but so that we may bring all of human life with us. In one sense Christ's offering is complete; in another it will not be complete until, through the Church which is his own Body, he has brought all of creation into subjection to his Father.

The Church's self-offering takes place in the daily lives of its members, as we offer ourselves to God and to our neighbours in acts of love and justice and mercy and goodness. But the place where this offering is identified as Christian, as having its foundation and its end in Christ, is when we meet together as a visible body to worship the Lord. It is in the Church's liturgy, above all in the sacrament of the Eucharist, that Christ makes himself present and knowable to his people as their great High Priest — the High Priest through whom we have access to God and may offer our lives to him.

Herein lies the theological foundation of the liturgical ministry of those who are called and appointed by Christ to preside over the celebration of his Word and sacraments. The reason why the ordained ministry, particularly the ministry of bishops and presbyters, may, not improperly, be called priestly is that through their ministry the Holy Spirit makes the fruits of Christ's own priesthood present and effective to his people. Through the ministry entrusted to those who are ordained — the ministry of the Eucharist, the ministry of baptism and reconciliation, the ministry of the Word, none of which a man or woman can celebrate alone, all of which require the presence of at least two or three meeting in the Lord's name — the risen and ascended Christ makes himself present to his people as their great High Priest who lives for ever to intercede for us.

Accordingly, those who are appointed to a priestly or diaconal ministry are called to speak and act — not only in church, but especially in church — not in their own name, but in the name of the Lord and of his Body. They have a role which, like every role, imposes its constraints.

There are the constraints of catholicity. What is said and done in common worship must be a proclamation and celebration not of ourselves but of the Gospel entrusted by Christ to his apostles and transmitted to us through the life of the Church. What we do today must be in recognizable continuity with the past which we have inherited.

There are the constraints of communion. What is said and done by one group of Christians must be recognizable to other Christians as an authentic proclamation and celebration of the one faith which is confessed by all.

The Church's liturgy is a drama which is not the private property of any particular individual or group. It is the common possession of the whole people of God. We are not free simply to make up the texts and the actions. At the same time, if our celebrations are not to be merely antiquarian, the texts, the stage-directions and the staging must always be open to renewal and adaptation in response to the constraints of the historical, social and physical situation of each particular community. As with a classical play, no two productions, if they are to live, will ever be precisely the same, nor will they be mere reconstructions of a past that is gone for ever. It is the task of liturgists, both experts and practitioners, to enable believers to experience themselves here and now as members of the one people of God. The texts are important. As with all poetry, there must be a proper precision of word and image. Place, setting and ritual are important. Liturgy, like all drama, is more than a matter of reading the words. It is an event in time and in space.

Already many of the Churches of the West are assimilating the work of liturgical revision that went on in the 1960s and 1970s. This process needs to be undertaken with a critical ear as to how new texts are being used and heard by local congregations; how images in particular prayers and the shape of whole services are being experienced and could be enriched for the coming generation.

Those who preside over liturgy need to be helped to accept and understand their role as, so to speak, actor-managers. Because the liturgy is the possession of the whole people, they must recognize the importance of association and memory. They are to organize the drama in such a way that all can be participants — remembering of course that people do not necessarily have to be talking all the time in order to participate. People are helped above all if they are enabled to pray, to forget themselves in their identity as children of God. They must be given space. They should not be overwhelmed or excluded. The only thing by which anyone may be excluded is the scandal of the cross.

To perform this ministry, those who are responsible need above all to understand what the drama is about. It is not to enable people to run away from the world. There can be no place for fantasy religion. Religion is real only if it connects the real world with the real God. The ministry of the liturgist is one of helping people to bring their real lives, their real world, our world, to God — with its pains and sorrows and its failures as well as its joys and thanksgivings. It is to help them to bring their world to God and find it transformed by his grace into a foretaste of heaven; to help them to receive the divine life in such a way that they can go back into their daily lives renewed — so that, having gone out into the world, they can bring it back again. If the power of Christ's sacrifice is truly proclaimed and known in the Church's liturgy, then it is the supreme means by which Christ, lifted up on the cross, draws the world to himself and so to his Father.

The end of it all is this, that when all things are subjected to God in Christ, God himself shall be 'all and in all' (1 Cor. 15.28). This hope, that in Christ heaven and earth shall be one, and God be all in all — this is the hope we celebrate every time we meet together in the name of the Lord and by the power of his Spirit lift up our hearts to heaven, that with angels and saints we may sing and praise his name: 'Holy, holy, holy is the Lord God of hosts, who was and is and is to come! Heaven and earth are full of his glory!'

2

The Christian Year

MICHAEL PERHAM

I

The Saturday newspapers often tell us the name of the following Sunday. 'Tomorrow's Services: The Sunday next before Lent', I read quite recently. It was true. It was going to be the Sunday next before Lent, but when I went over to church next morning it was to use the Prayer Book propers of 'Quinquagesima' and later in the morning the ASB propers of 'The Seventh Sunday before Easter'. Had I phoned Fr Bennett down the road at St Mary's, I would have found that he, following his Church's calendar, was keeping 'The Eighth Sunday of the Year'. A quick phone call to Anglican friends in Canada reveals that they are celebrating 'The Eighth Sunday after Epiphany'. It must be confusing for diary compilers and for those who do the Sunday services in the Saturday papers. For it is confusing to me, and unhelpful, I fear, to most churchgoers.

There are days when we all seem to be agreed, at least in the West, but they are few and far between. There seems little hope of a universal calendar by the year 2000, or even a Western agreed calendar, and, in any case, perhaps that is quite an unnecessary piece of uniformity. But some agreement either among denominations in England, or among Anglican provinces around the world, would seem both desirable and possible. In arguing for some changes in the Church of England calendar in the year 2000, I am not suggesting that we should go it alone, with our own eccentric calendar, but that this be a matter on which we should move forward in consultation with our partners.

Does it matter that we should get the calendar right? At one level the very untidiness of it is witness to its continuing development and its response to differing circumstances. In some ways the ironing out of oddities — like the delightfully named 'Septuagesima', 'Sexagesima' and 'Quinquagesima' Sundays — takes the fun out of the Christian calendar. Wasn't the 1970s' attempt to make everything neat, by moving the Annunciation from March to December, and the Trans-figuration from August to March, just the kind of tidying up that undermines the subtlety of the Christian year, with all its undercurrents and creative coincidences? [1]

It does matter that there should be coherence to the calendar, that people should be able to make sense of it, and that it should affirm, rather than cut across, theological and liturgical truths that we want to celebrate, but without the loss of those subtleties that relate one great Christian mystery to another. It does matter, because the rhythm of the liturgical year needs to be deep within us, so that its cycle of moods and seasons, high points and low, can interact with our own emotional experience, and help us relate, to deepen and to grow.

ASB 1980 marked an important breakthrough in the celebration of the liturgical year in the Church of England, for it provided the freedom in which each season could be given its distinctive emphasis and mood. The Book of Common Prayer celebrates the contrasting seasons only through collect and lections and, very occasionally, proper preface at the Eucharist. ASB 1980 allows for a greater richness and, at several points, provides the material for it. It has waited until the publication of *Lent, Holy Week, Easter* (1984)[2] and *The Promise of His Glory* (1990)[3] for the potential of the liturgical cycle to be spelt out and made readily accessible.

But, though the ASB includes a much richer provision of

10

seasonal material than previously, there are areas of calendrical confusion which need to be re-examined.

The most serious one is in its treatment of the Feast of Pentecost, where it has ended up with an unhappy compromise. In its provision of special texts (Opening Greeting, Peace, Invitation to Communion, Dismissal) for use 'from Easter Day to Pentecost', it reveals an understanding of the integrity of the fifty-days season that runs from Easter Day to Pentecost, taking in Ascension Day on the way. It is a season where the Feast of Pentecost is both the last day of the festival and also a special day celebrating the final strand of the Easter mystery — the gift of the Spirit — ending the festival period on a 'high'. (Epiphany or Candlemas do the same for the incarnation cycle, but see below.) If Pentecost is understood in this way, lections and other liturgical material that prepare for the celebration of the gift of the Spirit will be provided in the period from Ascension Day until Pentecost. On Pentecost evening, the last 'Alleluia' of the season dies away, the paschal candle is extinguished and we return, next morning, to a 'green' season of 'ordinary time'. But here the ASB compromises with the Prayer Book tradition and has a kind of Week of the Spirit (an octave minus a day) tacked on to the end of the fifty days. It is confused and confusing, and, unfortunately, *Lent, Holy Week, Easter* does nothing to solve it.[4]

Here it is a pity that we did not learn from the Roman calendar, which is unambiguous at this point, and, wisely, names the Sundays between Easter Day and Pentecost 'Sundays *of* Easter'. 'Sundays *after*' is unfortunate. But, at another point, the ASB was wise in avoiding Roman unambiguity. For it is one of the weaknesses of the present Roman calendar that, in the period after Christmas, it opted for a short Epiphany season and a return to 'ordinary time' straight after the Feast of the Lord's Baptism. The ASB, admittedly rather half-heartedly, tried to give the weeks of January a sense of being '*of*' Epiphany, with themes, preface, etc. that kept the revelation of Christ's glory before the faithful. A future calendar revision needs to take that one stage further, recognize the pivotal place occupied by Candlemas in the Christian year, and restore, in effect, a forty-day Christmas.

The third area of confusion has been in the experiment of a longer Advent, but one that introduced a series of Old Testament themes that ill accorded both with the traditional Advent themes and with the other days that Christians are keeping at this time of the year: All Saints' Day and Remembrance Sunday for nearly all, the Commemoration of the Faithful Departed (All Souls' Day) for some, and Christ the King for a few.

Whereas *Lent, Holy Week, Easter* left the ASB's calendrical confusion from Easter to Pentecost unresolved, *The Promise of His Glory* has faced the contradictions of the pre- and post-Christmas season, and brought an integrity and cohesion to the whole period from All Saints to Candlemas that will need to shape the calendar for that part of the year in any new service book. The Liturgical Commission now needs to be encouraged to apply the same rigorous thinking to the rest of the year, in relation both to the Easter festival and to 'ordinary time'.

Our use of 'ordinary time' and our nomenclature for it certainly needs re-examination as much as the festival periods. There is the short period between the Presentation and Ash Wednesday, and the longer period between Pentecost and All Saints' Day that need to be well used. The ASB's solution has been a heavily thematic approach, just as other calendars and lectionaries have sometimes gone for blocks of material through the summer months.[5] 'Ordinary time', for all that it is a new phrase to Anglican ears, is appealing if it means a period when the Church does not impose a theme on a local congregation. In ordinary time we are best set free either to read the

Scriptures sequentially, and allow them to speak for themselves without preordained theme, or to choose blocks of Scripture and series of themes that are tailor-made to the needs of the local church at that time. Providing that we return to a common lectionary around the great feasts, this kind of freedom must surely be welcomed. Should we not move into an area where there are 'closed' and 'open' seasons as far as local lectionary compilation is concerned?

If we are to do so, it will be important that the names we give to Sundays and the collects we provide for them do not begin to dictate themes. There needs to be a neutral tone to them, though we should resist the Roman 'Sundays of the Year', which is both prosaic and misleading. How, at one level, can the 'Tenth Sunday of the Year' be in May?

There are three further issues regarding the *temporale* that need to be examined.

The first is the transfer of great festivals to the nearest Sunday. Neither the BCP nor the ASB permits the transfer of, for instance, Epiphany, or Ascension Day or All Saints' Day to a Sunday, though the ASB goes some way in that direction by providing the Epiphany and Ascension *stories* on the nearest Sunday, as well as on the feast itself. Roman practice now encourages these transfers. More recently, *Lent, Holy Week, Easter* has allowed the possibility of the transfer of the Ash Wednesday rite to the First Sunday in Lent. *The Promise of His Glory* encourages the idea of Sunday observance in relation to All Saints' Day and the Presentation. What should a new service book advocate?

It is difficult to decide. It is clear that pastorally there is a strong argument for Sunday observance of a number of principal festivals. Without a transfer to a Sunday, the majority of churchpeople in most parishes will simply not share in these great festivals. In a new book a permissive transfer to the

13

Sunday seems almost inevitable for The Epiphany, The Presentation, The Ascension and All Saints' Day, at very least. But there are arguments against.

The argument against too many holy days superimposed, so to speak, on Sundays, is that they destroy the liturgical cycle and undermine Sunday as the weekly Day of the Resurrection — every Sunday as a 'little Easter'. This is the argument that prevails in the Roman calendar, and in the ASB calendar at certain times of the year, and transfers saints' days that land on a Sunday to the next or previous day.

If the principal concern is not to lose the liturgical cycle, though saints' days might do so, days like Epiphany, The Presentation, The Ascension and All Saints' Day can enhance that cycle, where a sympathetic lectionary is being followed.[6]

But the stronger argument against everything on Sunday is that it destroys the special character of different days by making them conform to the sameness of the Sunday Parish Communion slot. The liturgy of Christmas makes part of its impact by being in the middle of the night. Good Friday worship has something special about it around 3 o'clock. For many Christians Easter is never more powerful than when at daybreak. Some feast days cry out for celebration in the darkness, especially those winter feasts that use candlelight and speak of Christ as the Light. All Saints, Epiphany and, supremely, Candlemas call for a setting after dusk or before dawn. Ascension is a feast of the early morning or of midday. Something is lost when they all move to Sunday at 9.30 or 10 a.m. There is a good case for keeping these days where they belong, but ensuring that the liturgy to be celebrated for each is powerful enough to begin to draw people to church to celebrate them at times they have previously thought inconvenient.

This leads to a second question. What special liturgies for feast days and seasons should be included in a new book? *Lent, Holy Week, Easter* provided the Church of England with complete rites for Ash Wednesday, Palm Sunday, Maundy Thursday, Good Friday and Easter. Should they, in their entirety, find their way into a revised service book? It might just have seemed possible until *The Promise of His Glory* was published. For not only does that provide complete rites for All Saints' Day, All Souls' Day, Christmas, Epiphany and Candlemas, but it also introduces rich sets of proper material for every feast, fast and season within the three months of the year it celebrates, and so makes it inevitable that welcome provision will follow to supplement *Lent, Holy Week, Easter*, and to enrich the celebration of festivals not included in either book.[7] The quantity and quality of the material will surely point to a future supplementary book, entitled 'The Christian Year' or something like it, that will combine the two existing books and draw in other material, so that the whole year may be as well served as All Saints to Candlemas now is by *The Promise of His Glory*.

The third question concerns Saturday evenings and the eves of festivals. Ever since E. C. Ratcliff wrote about the subject for the Lambeth Conference in 1958,[8] Anglican opinion has been against two Evening Prayers for a Sunday or a festival, one on the eve, one on the day. ASB assumes one, and that one on the day, but allows it to be on the eve. Rome retains two Evening Prayers, and *The Promise of His Glory* sends strong signals in the same direction. The move to one Evening Prayer was a move to a greater simplicity in the calendar (first Evensongs being part of a world of complicated rules that confused the liturgical cycle) and a desire to be logical. As Jasper and Bradshaw put it:

According to Western practice, where a day runs from midnight to midnight, Evensong would be the last liturgical observance of the day: but according to Jewish practice, where a day runs from dusk to dusk, Evensong would be the first liturgical observance of the day. Over the centuries these two concepts came to be confused.[9]

But it is entirely natural, on the eve of a Sunday or a festival, to prepare for it, with readings, psalms, songs and prayers that introduce it. *The Promise of His Glory* provides a form of vigil service for Saturday nights and other eves of festivals, which includes a *Lucernarium* and concludes with the reading of the Gospel of the following day. To meet on Saturday night to say Evening Prayer without any thought of the worship of tomorrow is foolish. Evening Prayer of the night before needs encouragement.

But equally it is natural also, at the end of a Sunday or a festival, to come back, give thanks for the day and conclude its celebration. We do not have such short liturgical memories that we want to be on to the next thing before the day is out. Evening Prayer to prepare for a feast and Evening Prayer to round it off is not a confusion, but good psychology and good liturgy!

II

I turn now to the *sanctorale*, the celebration of the saints in the Christian year. I cannot imagine that this will be an area of radical change, and for most people it is fairly unimportant whether, for instance, St Ambrose be celebrated in April or December, and whether he should have a 'full service' or just a mention in the Intercession Prayers! But I would make five pleas.

Firstly, I would argue for the retention of some festivals at apparently silly times. I would not argue for keeping everything just where it is (I am glad, for instance, that I no longer have to celebrate St Matthias the very next day after launching into Lent, as I found myself doing with the Prayer Book calendar in Winchester Cathedral in 1982). But I do believe that some feast days always have had, or have acquired, a deep significance simply by being apparently in the wrong place. St Stephen, St John and the Holy Innocents add something very important to our Christmas theology by being where they are on 26, 27 and 28 December, and we should not follow the Canadian *Book of Alternative Services* and rob them of their subtlety by scattering them to January, May and August. The Annunciation may be on 25 March because it is nine months before Christmas, but the figure of Mary pulled into the foreground for a day just as Lent builds up to Holy Week, with the thought of her obedience, first expressed in the Annunciation, reaching its climax at the foot of the cross, provides the kind of undercurrent from which good liturgy is made. Iron it out of March and introduce it in December and all that is lost. The Transfiguration does indeed belong to the same build-up to the passion, but, celebrate it on 6 August, and not only does it take on a new dimension in high summer, where sunlight and Christ's glory meet one another, but it also draws in the Hiroshima experience, also on 6 August, opening up another creative theological reflection about the nature of trans-figuration. All these examples are warnings against too ready a tidying up of the Christian year.

Nevertheless the second plea is for the integrity of seasons. The ASB gives no hint of how the character of a season is to be maintained. Advent and Lent in particular, but other seasons too, suffer from too many saints' days that interrupt the flow and feel of the season. *Lent, Holy Week, Easter* and *The Promise of His Glory* both caution against this, and those who revise the calendar do well to clear these seasons of saints' days except where either a strong cult is established — St David and St Patrick, for instance, in Lent — or the saint does not so much cut across the season as contribute to its character. *The Promise* suggests that St Nicholas and The Conception of Mary accord well with the feel of Advent. Equally both St Polycarp and St Perpetua, by their martyrs' witness for Christ, enhance the Lenten season, rather than detract from it.

One feast day needs particular rethinking. It is that of The Blessed Virgin Mary. It has an interesting recent history. The Liturgical Commission argued for a festival on 15 August in its 1976 report:

> We propose . . . a festival of the Blessed Virgin Mary on August 15. A festival of the Blessed Virgin on this date was first observed by the eastern Church in the early seventh century and was adopted by the western Church about a century later. It originally commemorated her death, as other saints' days commemorate the death of other saints, but later became associated under a variety of titles with doctrines that are not regarded as part of the Church of England's doctrine. However, the festival of the Annunciation is widely regarded as a festival of our Lord, and not of our Lady, and upon this understanding of the matter it follows that the Church of England has no festival of the Blessed Virgin herself. These considerations led us to agree that there ought to be a festival dedicated to the Blessed Virgin Mary, in her own right so to speak . . .[10]

But the General Synod debate changed the date from 15 August to 8 September, and this is the date given in the ASB. This is unfortunate, both because it gives a set of 'propers' that are about Mary's heavenly glory to be read on the day when other Christians celebrate her birth, rather than her death, and also because it puts us unnecessarily out of line with other Churches and with other provinces of our own Communion. It is just the kind of liturgical revision on 'the floor of the house' that gives the Synod a bad name.

Fourthly, I would plead for clearer criteria in choosing

names for inclusion in the calendar of saints. I have written about this in some detail in *The Communion of Saints*.[11] The haphazard way in which names were put in to the calendar of saints in the ASB, taken out, and restored, simply on the preference of Commission members, the Synod and the House of Bishops was almost inevitable, given the absence of any clear guidelines about how the Anglican Church recognizes and celebrates heroic sanctity. The most influential document has been *The Commemoration of Saints and Heroes of the Faith in the Anglican Communion* produced in preparation for the 1958 Lambeth Conference. But it is slim and inadequate.

A further point follows from this. The bald ASB statement that 'diocesan, local or other commemorations may be added to these lists' should be amplified to encourage the development of local supplementary calendars. This is not in order to produce esoteric lists of long-forgotten local saints with unpronounceable names, most of them queens, abbesses and virgins of the eighth century, but to explore the concept of heroic sanctity as we encounter it in the Church of today. Who are the people from earlier in the century whom Christians in different parts of the country remember as men and women of God? We know that in Lincoln they think of Edward King, and he indeed is the most modern 'saint' in the ASB calendar. But are there not others, and is it not their acceptance into diocesan and local calendars that begins a process by which they might be celebrated nationally if their story meets a response in a wider community? The 1957 report advocated a fifty-year rule: no consideration for inclusion in a calendar until fifty years had passed from their death. This does not stand easily alongside the idea of canonization as the spontaneous action of the community! By the year 2000 William Temple, but not George Bell, will be free of that questionable rule. But are the saints of the modern age all in episcopal orders? The commemoration of heroic sanctity needs a new look.

NOTES

1 See Henry de Candole, 'The Calendar', in Ronald Jasper, ed., *The Calendar and Lectionary*, Oxford, Clarendon Press, 1967.

2 *Lent, Holy Week, Easter: Services and Prayers*, Church House Publishing, Cambridge University Press and SPCK, 1986.

3 *The Promise of His Glory: Services for the Season from All Saints to Candlemas*, Synod edn GS 907, London, Church House Publishing, 1990.

4 See Michael Perham, *Liturgy Pastoral and Parochial* (London, SPCK, 1984), p. 102; and also Roger Greenacre and Jeremy Haselock, *The Sacrament of Easter* (Leominster, Gracewing, 1989), pp. 148–57.

5 See Martin Dudley, 'The Lectionary', in Michael Perham, ed., *Towards Liturgy 2000*, London, SPCK, 1989.

6 See Kenneth Stevenson and Michael Perham, *Welcoming the Light of Christ* (London, SPCK, 1990), pp. 102ff.

7 A book by Trevor Lloyd, Michael Perham and David Stancliffe to meet this need is in preparation.

8 In *The Commemoration of Saints and Heroes of the Faith in the Anglican Communion* (London, SPCK, 1957), pp. 81–3.

9 Ronald Jasper and Paul Bradshaw, *A Companion to The Alternative Service Book* (London, SPCK, 1986), p. 69.

10 *The Calendar, Lectionary and Rules to Order the Service*, A Report by the Liturgical Commission, GS 292 (London, SPCK, 1976), p. 6.

11 Michael Perham, *The Communion of Saints*, Alcuin Club Collections 62 (London, SPCK, 1980), pp. 121–41.

3

Eucharistic Inflation

DONALD GRAY

'Do we have too many Eucharists?' is a question which some have been asking in recent years. Is the current fashion that every parochial and diocesan event should be 'eucharistized' a right use of this great sacrament of the Church; or is it a convenience which is born out of what is thought to be currently right liturgically?

The situation arises because of the reassertion of the principle that the Eucharist is the definitive way in which the Church worships. The pioneers of the Parish Communion Movement quite rightly sought to restore the Eucharist to a central place in the worship patterns of the parish churches of England. In the eighteenth and the early nineteenth century, although the Eucharist had not ceased to be celebrated in the parish churches, it was never the main service of the day, even in the way the Book of Common Prayer presumed it would be.

When the Oxford Movement brought the Eucharist back into pre-eminence in many places up and down the country, it was always as a dual pattern. This consisted of an early celebration for communion and a later sung service for devotion. It was the latter which attracted the larger congregations. The advocates of the Parish Communion sought to bring these two services together into one service of worship and devotion at which there was a general communion of the congregation.[1]

Immediately before the 1939–45 War, and then with great

rapidity after the War, the Parish Communion displaced mid-morning Matins in those parishes which had that particular tradition, and also the mid-morning Sung Eucharist in churches of that style of churchmanship. There was great rejoicing among many that the Parish Communion had achieved what nothing else had hitherto seemed capable of: a breaking-down of the hard and fast barriers of churchmanship that too often had seemed capable of stultifying the mission of the Church of England.

The effect was a widely accepted parochial liturgical pattern which had no reference to 'high' or 'low' church inclinations. As a consequence the pattern of liturgical revision which occupied so much of the Church's energies in the period from 1960 to 1980 sought to provide material that served the needs of, what was by then, the majority of the parishes. *The Alternative Service Book 1980* assumed a Parish Communion parish.[2]

For the best part of forty-five years now, confirmation instruction, teaching sermons, parochial strategy have all attempted to produce a more eucharistically aware 'People of God'. At the same time there has been a corresponding decline in many places of some knowledge of the form and contents of those other basic services of Anglicanism — Matins and Evensong. And this is despite efforts to include elements such as psalms and canticles within the Eucharist.

It would be too foolish to represent the situation as one in which, all over England, congregations have unwillingly and unthinkingly drifted into a fashionable pattern. The growth of eucharistic worship has had the effect of deepening and informing the devotions of many thousands of Anglicans who, at the same time, discovered that by obeying the divine command to 'do this' they had also found a way into a heritage of spirituality which was as old as the Church itself. And this led them on to a further discovery.

The newly awakened and eucharistically aware Anglicans realized that they were now moving beyond not only the internal disputes of the Church of England, but on to a plane of shared and ecumenical understanding. The Liturgical Movement in the Roman Catholic Church had not needed to restore the Mass to a central place within the spirituality of the faithful, but rather had sought to emphasize the essential role of participation and involvement. The truth they had to rediscover was the high privilege of participation, not just of the priest, but of all those who were gathered around the altar of God. Equally the social and political implications of the eucharistic offering were re-found insights which also could be shared across the denominational boundaries, making the Eucharist profoundly something which could be seen as 'on earth as it is in heaven'.

This common growth in understanding was not confined to the Anglican/Roman Catholic axis of ecumenical sharing; the Eucharist was returning to 'the pole position' in the Churches of Protestant Nonconformity at the same time. The revised service books, which each of the major denominations in Britain has produced in recent years, bear eloquent testimony to this. In these books forms and orders for eucharistic worship, which earlier this century would not have been thought to be providing for any kind of pastoral necessity, occupy a primary position.[3]

Thus it seems as though the Church, in those places where it is active and aware, is becoming the eucharistic Church. But that apparent development has sounded warning bells for some! Without necessarily denying the definitive place of the Eucharist in Christian worship or disturbing the vision of all the faithful gathering around the Table of the Lord, some have questioned the wisdom of putting all our liturgical eggs into only one pastoral basket.

The critics of the 'Eucharist with everything' approach

would seem to divide into two camps (with, of course, all the usual overlaps that such a precise categorization risks). There are those who look back to the days of a fairly widespread pattern of Morning Prayer and Evening Prayer, Sunday by Sunday, in many churches, and they suggest that such services were available and acceptable for those who might attend church with only a fairly low level of commitment. The Eucharist, they argue, is a service for the devout believer, not the casual dropper-in.

Against this, it is argued by those who defend a eucharistic pattern, there is the fact that if the Eucharist is the Christian offering of worship *par excellence*, and if it 'betokens and reveals the Church', then it is very important that this must be *the* service which should be available for the outsider to see and experience. Charles Wesley was quite convinced that the Eucharist was 'a converting ordinance', and said that many of his early converts could give testimony to that fact.

Surely the Church will inflict great damage on itself if it allows even the slightest suggestion that the Eucharist is only for 'the in-crowd', that it is reserved for the specially holy. What kind of role is the Church designing for itself when it seems to be taking the Eucharist away from the vulgar stare of the outsider in order to make it a hole-in-the-corner ceremony for the initiated? Isn't the ideal this: that the Church should so order its worship that it does not overwhelm the visitor, the casual dropper-in, but yet still provides a clear and coherent declaration, for those who would hear, of the truths of the gospel. Do the critics of such carefully ordered worship believe that the musical intricacies of Matins or Evensong, which are quite capable of flowing unheeded over many, are *more* able to trigger off a sense of the numinous than a well-ordered Eucharist?

Of course, in God's providence, they are quite capable of lifting up heart and mind and spirit, but the question is whether they do it better and more often. It is always possible to cite services in which either an overwhelming heartiness militates against any attempt at fairly anonymous participation, or where the order is of such gnostic and impenetrable complexity that none but the most carefully instructed would be likely to fathom its depths. But they must be the exception.

The second of the critical camps is occupied by those who would readily grant the impossibility of using Matins or Evensong for the occasional worshipper. These are they who are very anxious to provide 'a half-way house' for those who are either unwilling or hesitant about making the commitment which they believe (rightly or wrongly) is expected of them when they attend the Eucharist. These critics would also plead the cause of those who are deterred, under our present Church of England regulations, from any deeper involvement because of the requirement of being confirmed before becoming a regular communicant. Such 'a half-way house' has been reckoned to be provided by the Family Service (particularly where this is always a non-eucharistic service).

After a tradition of Church of England Liturgical Commissions setting their faces against providing any guidance on the subject of Family Services (with the exception of an only marginally useful pamphlet, *Family and Evangelistic Services*, published in 1967)[4] the present Liturgical Commission has changed that policy and has provided much useful material for this kind of service in its recently published *Patterns for Worship*. Stimulated by the not unfair criticisms voiced in *Faith in the City* of the impossibility of inner-city congregations wading their way through the nearly 1300 closely-packed pages of liturgical material contained in ASB, the Commission has now provided both the skeletons, and the wherewithal to clothe them, for what it chooses to call 'Services of the Word' in its report. Coaching hints, and the possibility of the production of carefully designed and illustrated booklets in the future, make it possible to contemplate the provision of attractive, accessible worship which would not necessarily deter either the inquirer, or the mildly interested parent, who might find themselves accompanying children to what is probably still called in the parish 'A Family Service'.[5]

In the outlines provided by the Commission, some of them are in fact intended for a Eucharist, while others use *inter alia* material derived from the eucharistic sections. This would seem to be a wise attempt to deal with the obvious problem inherent in Family Services: when, and at what point, is the regular worshipper at that service encouraged to move on to the Parish Communion? A growing familiarization with parts of the Eucharist would assist in this process.

It is good news that the Church of England seems now to have passed beyond the point where it lacked the confidence to provide orders for Family Services, in case they militated against our carefully designed provisions for the Eucharist. We have been convinced both by the paucity of material currently available, and the seeming lack of imagination in the ways in which it might possibly be used. We have long poured scorn on 'the hymn sandwich' and yet have produced what was little better than that deservedly despised format for many Family Services. Equally we have, at last, realized the potentiality of worship as a means of evangelism, not in order that it might be a continual force-feeding of the challenge of the gospel, but so that it can be a demonstration of the *koinonia* of the Church and a sharing of the sense of the joy in believing.

In the aftermath of the 1939–45 War the Church in France realized that it needed something which might go alongside the regular worship of the parishes. For these forms of worship the Roman Catholic Liturgical Movement invented the phrase 'para-liturgies'.[6]

In the present 'missionary' situation in England there would seem to be a real need for such imaginative liturgies which would be capable of stimulating interest and provoking questions, while not necessarily answering them. We must always beware of liturgy becoming educative. We do not need to create congregations which leave church asking, 'What have I learnt today?'.

The opportunities provided by Services of the Word, and para-liturgies, must be grasped, and the Church must not be backward in providing models and materials for them. We do not need to assume that such materials will be necessarily contained within ASB 2000. That book would perhaps include the skeletons, but the supply of other materials would be maintained in other forms. However, for the preparation of them we should use our best liturgists. It should not just be left to private enterprise to provide. The Church should demonstrate its seriousness about this matter by using official resources in its production. We should not lose sight of the possibility that some of this material could be useful to even the most settled and instructed congregations as an addition to their normal liturgical menu.

Yet all this must not be at the expense of driving the Eucharist underground into ghettos inhabited by the specially informed, the first-class and higher-grade Christians. The Eucharist will always be the best and most perfect means of showing what the Church is, and what Christian worship is at its best. It does not need to be protected by us, we are not its keepers, the Lord of the Church will guard his own.

It is more a question of tactics. There will always be the right time when the Eucharist is the best expression of the Church's message, when nothing else can 'speak' as loudly and as clearly. That will not necessarily, by any stretch of the imagination, be just for 'church' occasions or when there are no 'outsiders' present. Equally, there will be times (perhaps more often than we now imagine) when the Church does not need to feel that it can only do the Eucharist to mark some point in its life or history. Wise pastoral judgement allied to shrewd liturgical insights will help to make the decision.

Inflation is not the same as devaluation; devaluation does not always follow inflation. A wise Church will draw from its liturgical treasury things new and old, but the wisdom will be shown in what it uses — and when.

NOTES

1 Alf Härdelin, *The Tractarian Understanding of the Eucharist*, Studia Historico-Ecclesiastica Uppsaliensia 8 (Uppsala, University Press, 1965), pp. 278ff.

2 Donald Gray, *Earth and Altar, The Evolution of the Parish Communion in the Church of England to 1945*, Alcuin Club Collections 68 (Norwich, Canterbury Press, 1968), pp. 3–6 and *passim*.

3 Ronald C. D. Jasper, ed., *The Renewal of Worship*, Essays by Members of the Joint Liturgical Group (London, SPCK, 1965), pp. 3–12.

4 In 1981 the Alcuin Club produced a more useful guide in Kenneth Stevenson, *Family Services*, Alcuin Club Manual No. 3.

5 *Patterns for Worship*, A Report by the Liturgical Commission of the General Synod of the Church of England, GS 898 (London, Church House Publishing, 1989), pp. 4–5.

6 Ernest Benjamin Koenker, *The Liturgical Renaissance in the Roman Catholic Church* (Chicago 1954), pp. 55–6.

4

Soft Points in the Eucharist

KENNETH STEVENSON

I

A title like that evokes the immediate question, 'What is a "soft point"?'. The answer is easy.

Robert Taft is probably the most distinguished liturgical scholar in the Roman Catholic Church today. A specialist in the Eastern rites, he has written extensively on the way in which liturgies develop. He invariably has an eye on the present — he is not so engrossed in what happened (or didn't) in fourth-century Syria that he forgets the needs of today's Church. And when he writes about his own Church, much of what he has to say affects the revised rites of many other Christian communions, including our own.

In an illuminating essay on the way the Byzantine Liturgy evolved, Taft[1] identifies three stages which are characterized by 'actions without words', and where history shows that different eucharistic rites are prone to spontaneous and sometimes ephemeral growth. These are (1) the entrance into church, (2) the preparation of the gifts, and (3) the fraction, communion, and dismissal rites. It is at these points that the Byzantine (and other) rites experienced most cluttering of material, responding to pastoral and choreographic needs. And these are precisely the stages in the ASB Rite A where further revision is needed, because what we have already is fine and good, but the process of revision needs to go that bit further in order to provide a clearer and more devotionally balanced liturgy.

In one sense, it is easy to see why these three 'soft points' have emerged in the way they have. The drift of twentieth-century liturgical scholarship, immortalized in Gregory Dix's *The Shape of the Liturgy,*[2] has resulted in an approach to the history of the Eucharist that identifies the three 'strata' of the service. In order to clarify my argument, it is perhaps worth summarizing the Dix 'thesis' since it has been so influential on all revision that has taken place, and has also won the admiration of generations of scholars.

Stratum I is the early core of the service, the one which is discernible from the writings of Justin Martyr, and others. All we have are the 'deep structures' of the Eucharist, the shape that has generally survived even the most savage of revision processes. It consists of the following:

> Readings (with chants)
> Homily
> Prayers
> Peace
> (functional preparation of the table)
> Thanksgiving
> Communion

Any modern service book illuminates that basic core of material and modern Christians owe an enormous debt of gratitude to the people responsible for the various revisions. The new Roman *Ordo Missae* is based round that ground-plan. But there is more than stratum I, for stratum II comes along (in the fourth century) and shifts that simple structure from a pre-Nicene house-church into a new environment, a basilica. Its additions include the 'soft points' we noted earlier, and they are as follows:

> Introit chant (responsorial or choral)
> Collect

Readings (increasingly systematized)
Homily
Prayers (beginning to drop out)
Peace
(elaborate preparation of table for large crowd)
Thanksgiving (developing intercessions)
Preparation of consecrated gifts for communion
Communion
Concluding rite

Such a pattern gives us the bare bones of many a modern Parish Communion, though it should be noted, too, that those who were not baptized were dismissed before the Peace. Stratum II is not, however, the end of the story, for the Western Eucharist migrated not only from the house-church into the basilica, it also, later on, in the time of Charlemagne, spread from that grandiose setting into the quiet, devotional milieu of the side-altar Low Mass, often with only the priest and the server, and perhaps a few others, depending on the circumstances. The Eucharist now has to include a recurring backdrop for the prayers of the priest. That is exactly what 'stratum III' comes along and achieves:

Private prayers in sacristy during vesting
Private prayers at the foot of the altar
Kyrie or Gloria (said)
Collect
Readings (only two now)
Creed (on certain occasions)
Private prayers at the preparation of the gifts
Thanksgiving (mostly silent)
Private prayers before, during and after communion
Concluding rite
Private prayers (including Last Gospel) on way to sacristy.

The genius of the Eucharist lies in its capacity to adapt to new circumstances, and that is precisely what it does in this new setting. Subsequent developments bring the devout worshipper into that service, with devotional preaching, often making the Mass itself an allegory of the life (or passion) of Christ. And the Reformers come along in the sixteenth century and sweep a good deal away in the interests of bringing the Lord's Supper back to its pristine simplicity; and (as we know) their knowledge of things ancient was not as developed as ours for the simple reason that a lot of the early evidence was lost or neglected.[3] It has only been in the last hundred years that it has come to light again, in order to serve both scholarship and the move towards revision. But that is another story.

What, then, can this illuminating tale tell us about the revision of Rite A? It can tell us a great deal, because it informs us about how the Eucharist can migrate from one environment into another, with a particular kind of 'norm' or 'house-style' dominating a particular age and therefore imposing itself on the rest. Today's norm is the main Sunday morning Eucharist of a parish church, and that is why the service has been structured the way it has, with a musical introit, a participatory rite at the presentation of the gifts, and a collective concluding rite. Following the Reformation fad for penitential prayer, the confession has been kept and sharpened in focus, but with the option that it can take place at the beginning or just before the Peace. How should this be revised?

I would like to look at this issue in two ways. First, Rite A as it stands contains some good material, but not always well-arranged, at the 'soft point' outlined earlier and sketched above. The Introit is a good candidate for closer inspection. Typographically, this is described as 'The Preparation', and it thus sits on the same level as 'The Ministry of the Word' and 'The Ministry of the Sacrament'. That in itself is good pastoral liturgy, since people today need to learn that preparing for worship is as important as the worship itself. (In the oft-repeated words of Archbishop William Temple, 'If you are going to pray for ten minutes, you spend the first eight getting ready!') But this 'Preparation' contains so much that it suffers from the cluttering effect of so many other 'soft points'. In some of the Eastern rites, the process becomes prolonged and confused. And we really do need to be told *why* the Confession can come in two different positions. I have often told congregations that if it comes right at the start, it is a preparation for worship, and the whole Eucharist (as the Roman rite makes plain, 'in order to prepare ourselves to celebrate these holy mysteries, let us call to mind our sins'), whereas if it comes later on, it is a preparation of the communicants for coming to the Lord's Table. That may be a false mystagogy, but my circumstances (having to use Rite A regularly) have forced me to articulate it. The act of penitence, for all that it is a relative latecomer to the Western Eucharist, has proved remarkably adhesive to the rite. It has survived revisions and is a common feature in all modern service books. This may stem in part from the fact that it has all the signs of a strong liturgical unit, made up of bidding, confession, and absolution, a unit, moreover, with a distinct purpose. But it has to be said that when it comes in the later position *and is followed* by the prayer of humble access, the congregation may be getting rather too much of a good thing. The prayer of humble access owes its liturgical genre to the late medieval vernacular devotions, which is one of the reasons why it works hard, and not always successfully, to find a viable place in modern liturgies.

Another critical feature of the 'preparation' is the fact that it often contains what seems too much music. The *Gloria in excelsis* comes soon after a rousing introit hymn, which it was never originally intended to do. Some of these issues need resolution somehow.

The second 'soft point' centres round the preparation of the gifts, and in Rite A this is the most confused and confusing of all, because not only are we envisaging different styles of celebration, we are also entering an area where different theologies operate. The original drafters of Series 3 produced a neat and simple form at this point, but the politics of revision and other pressures soon complicated things. (If it is any comfort to the original Liturgical Commission, exactly the same story took place in Rome, as anyone who compares the 1965 draft *Missa normativa* with the 1970 Missal can tell!)

The theological issue is the question of in what sense is the preparation of the gifts a functional act, in what sense symbolic; and it centres round attitudes and language of offering. Evangelicals tend to be nervous about the language of offering, remembering in their corporate consciousness the old medieval private prayers at this point, which were loaded with sacrificial language. Anglo-Catholics, many of them sympathetic to the protest, look at the 1970 Missal and see the kind of simplified offertory rite and prayers that say exactly what they think they mean at this point in the service. Others again shun the Evangelical sensitivity and the Anglo-Catholic enthusiasm and want a simpler rite that places the gifts symbolically on the table, and a richer eucharistic prayer that speaks of the Eucharist as a spiritual sacrifice in stronger terms than Rite A.[4] And there will be yet others with different points of view, for that is the nature of Anglicanism on the ground.

But if you look at the dreaded page 129 of the ASB, you will see that you can do just about anything, and, worst of all, you can prepare the gifts having said the optional Roman offertory prayers ('Blessed are you . . .'), and *after* that, and *before* the eucharistic prayer, you can sing a hymn, which seems to be an act that throws right out of focus what the offertory is, and lays you open to the charge of exaggerating the preparation of the gifts. The matter is complicated further by the fact that the

'Yours, Lord' (1 Chron. 29.11) prayer is to be said over the 'offerings of the people'.[5]

Clearly such an amalgam of words and actions is laying the whole rite open to a cluster of different kinds of uses, many of them reflecting what people have been doing for some time. A revision of Rite A should set about clearing up some of the muddled thinking and action, by a process of education, simplification, and then providing a better libretto that is acceptable to all sides. I would suggest a tougher approach to the use of the hymn, so that it never *follows* the preparation of the bread and wine; simpler directions that do not try to drive a wedge between the presentation of the bread and wine, and that of the offerings of the people; and an offertory prayer that brings together fairly and squarely the sixteenth-century Reformation sensitivity about justification by faith, and the twentieth-century awareness of ecology and the sacraments. As it happens, the American *Lutheran Book of Worship* provides us with an eloquent (if prolix) example:

> Blessed are you, O Lord our God,
> maker of all things.
> Through your goodness you have blessed us
> with these gifts.
> With them we offer ourselves to your service
> and dedicate our lives to the care and redemption
> of all that you have made, for the sake of him
> who gave himself for us, Jesus Christ our Lord.[6]

Many clergy are a little wary of the offertory, with its elaborate processions, and sometimes even pompous movement of important people carrying bread or wine, or loads of cash, to the Lord's Table. Whatever is *said* (and as a sceptic about *this* aspect of offering I appreciate that something does need to be said, if only at the big sung celebrations), it should bring home to people the essentially *incomplete* nature of this part of the service. It is not a self-assertion, nor yet what Michael Ramsey immortalized in the oft-quoted words, 'a shallow and Romantic sort of Pelagianism'[7] (words of which Ramsey remained blissfully impenitent to the end of his days). But it is an act that gives many a eucharistic president the 'itch' to say something. I may not be alone in feeling that something should be said, but that we have not quite reached the appropriate form.

Before leaving the problematic offertory, it is perhaps worth drawing attention to another failure of the revisers in connection with the actions of the president. Just before the eucharistic prayer starts, the president is supposed to 'take' the bread and wine, the implication being that they will not be touched during the prayer itself. Many people doubt whether this is good theology, or good theatre, and the verdict on this action must, for the time being, remain an open one.

The third 'soft point' is the last one, centring around the material immediately before and after communion. In many respects, what we have functions well, although there are many places where elaborate settings of the *Agnus Dei* are sung during the communion itself, which does not go against the spirit of the rite. *Patterns for Worship* contains several variable responses at the breaking of the bread. These have not been drafted in order to bring variety to the service for its own sake. Many would like to see the fraction (or at least the initial breaking) done in silence. ('We break this bread' does seem to be wearing a little thin.) This would be followed by one or other of a series of variable prayers, such as the following, based on well-known words from the *Didache*:

> Creator of all,
> we have gathered many grains
> and made them into this one bread.

(All) We look for your Church to be gathered

from the ends of the earth
into the Kingdom.[8]

It is in the conclusion of the service that some of the same
problems occur as at the beginning. Many people say that Rite
A ends abruptly, though this is a feature others would praise,
as being in line with the spirit of the old 'Series 2' service, with
its 'after the vision, the task' spirituality. However, perhaps we
need an alternative structure, with not just variable post-
communion prayers, but some congregational acclamation,
along the lines of the 1985 Canadian *Book of Alternative
Services.*[9] The move from blessing to dismissal has always been
sharp, and it may be the reason why the dismissal, though much
older than the blessing, has found it hard to coexist with it.

II

My second look at these 'soft points' has the purpose of
relating the previous history to the present service, in other
words, to match Taft and Dix with Rite A's problems and
possibilities. This involves taking into account not just what
Rite A says, but how it is actually done. Liturgists need to take
far more seriously the way in which rubrics and directions
develop, and their often flagrantly contrasting relationship
with pastoral practice. It need hardly be added that ours is by
no means the first generation to experience such a dichotomy.

The 'preparation' is of far greater importance and involves
far greater diversity of practice than many of us realize. When
I first started teaching liturgy, I used to take the Dix line at its
most literal, namely that the Eucharist comes in two parts,
Word and Sacrament. But in recent years, I have come to view
the Rite A division of the Eucharist into the *three* parts, of
Preparation, Word, and Sacrament, far more seriously, not

because of its grounding in history, but because it makes so much more pastoral sense for our times.

What we need to do with the 'Preparation' is to stop regarding it as an agenda to be gone through, and to use it as a necessary and helpful feature of liturgy that requires different styles for the very varying environments in which the Eucharist is celebrated. Thus, a choral festal celebration will inevitably contain a lot of music, and that music will form the congregation's own preparation, of a corporate kind. For that kind of service, surely, material such as the Collect for purity, and even the Summary of the Law and the Confession (perhaps) could either become the private devotional preparation of the congregation, before the service starts, or form a rite of preparation by a deacon beforehand. On the other hand, a week-day liturgy needs to be simple and quiet, in which the Kyrie, in an extended form, could be the basis for the Confession. (Examples of the latter are to be found in *Patterns for Worship*.)[10] Yet again, there will be places in which the start of the service is dominated by what is sometimes called the 'chorus culture', in which spontaneous songs are the congregation's approach to worship, and serve the function of gathering disparate feelings and thoughts into a corporate focus. In that setting, it makes little sense to start the 'liturgy proper' at any other point than the Collect of the Day.

Then, the same observations operate with the 'Preparation of the gifts'. It is impossible to expect the sung celebration to function in the same way as a House Communion. For that reason, we need fewer mandatory directions, and more scope for a variety of suggestions as to how these might be implemented. For example, a corporate Sunday Eucharist needs a sense of rhythm about it, and most congregations will expect it. For that reason, people do not want to be led through a complex series of ritual actions by priest and servers, without having some kind of explanation. On the other hand, the celebration of the Eucharist at the end of a House Group may well include the 'offering' of tokens and thoughts that have been prominent in the discussion and reflection on that particular occasion. (It could also be linked to the notion of prayer as sacrifice, of which I have written elsewhere.)[11] What we *don't* want to do is to multiply the complexities that are already apparent under the surface of Rite A at this point. I have watched fussy offertory processions, even those that interrupt the hymn with an intercalated prayer (!), and compared the experience with watching a Danish Lutheran pastor pour wine from a large and generous flagon into a commodious and well-designed altar chalice. Conservative Evangelicals have something to teach the rest of us about liturgical reticence. A revised Rite A could do much worse than start with the simple pattern outlined in the BCP (1979) of the American Episcopal Church.[12]

Similar fruit can be gleaned from the final 'soft point' of the Eucharist, for it is here that the variety of context and style is actually brought home with far greater force to the communicants themselves. We are already experiencing something of the need to relate symbolism to reality over eucharistic bread, as witness the number of companies now producing wafer-bread that looks more and more like 'ordinary bread'. We are distributing communion to great crowds by the most primitive and convenient method of all — standing. We are also learning that it is unsightly (and, to the liturgically uneducated, irreverent) to watch clergy and ministers gulp down the remains at the end of the communion in the sight of all. These are areas where the official text needs further and much firmer supplementary directions, or suggestions, rather than leaving them to the whim of local culture, or the chance good idea given by an expert at a clergy conference. Style of celebration, too, can determine the way in which a liturgy 'winds down'. Some people are reacting against the spirituality of the abrupt dismissal — they want to linger in the temple, whatever the keen-minded cleric has to say to the contrary. Some monastic communities have the Psalms of Terce after the Communion, forming a powerful devotional conclusion to the rite. Others again go so far as to lament the positioning of the *Gloria in excelsis* at the beginning, preferring Cranmer's final solution in 1552 by placing it at the end.[13] (It is quite possible to do this with Rite A under the present directions, as the *Gloria* may be omitted from its 'official' position at the start, and it may be classed as a 'hymn' to be sung after Communion.) I still wonder, in any case, whether the big rousing hymns that are often sung at the end of Eucharists do not fit better between the blessing and dismissal (where many communities place them anyway) than in the preferred position, immediately before the post-communion prayer. Much of this is to do with mood and function, and that is where a 'soft point' is particularly 'soft'.

III

Some of the foregoing remarks could be met by more imaginative use of what we already have, which is the cry of the liturgist down through the ages. But not all. Rite A is the result of the evolution of a particular liturgy at a particular time, within a carefully definable context. And no official liturgical libretto is going to be perfect. Indeed, one of the signs of strength in Rite A is the way in which it has brought the Church of England together, so that within a single, flexible text, many different groups can come together without the feeling of cultural shock. Nevertheless, we *are* a pluriform Church, and even within the same parish community there are going to be different styles and contexts, and it looks as if these divergences are going to proliferate for the foreseeable future. This is why it is necessary to examine afresh the way these three 'soft points' are being used, and what is really going on under the surface, and how a revised text, with supplementary suggestions, could both express the best of what is going on and nudge the wider Church on to better things. That sort of discussion is necessarily complex, and is in its own way as subtle and nuanced as discussions of other kinds, such as what should go into a eucharistic prayer. But it is just as important for the People of God.

There is one optional 'soft point' that might figure more prominently, to which I want to draw attention by way of postscript. It concerns what to do with the Gospel. In many places, the Liturgy of the Word can be flat and banal, and the kind of dignity that ought to be given to the reading of Scripture downgraded into what some would regard as a trivialization. The 'paperback' culture is everywhere, and I have seen well-intentioned gospel-readers slouch forward to proclaim the good news in as casual and muttered a way as possible. Perhaps to counteract this, and to give the gospel reading its own peculiar prominence, we could reach out to an old tradition of bringing the Book of the Gospels into church at the entrance and placing it on the altar, and carrying it down to the place where it is to be read from, with some appropriate solemnity. This, of course, brings in another question that requires its own special exploration, the interaction of president, deacon, and other ministers, within the whole community's worship. But it also cries out for a publisher to come forward and offer to print, perhaps in a limited edition, the texts of the four Gospels, *in their entirety*[14] (in an age when lections change, the ASB Altar Book with its many different versions of the Bible is not enough!), and bind them together in a suitably handsome form. That would give the Gospel's own potential 'soft point' an appropriate dignity.

NOTES

1   Robert F. Taft, 'How Liturgies Grow: The Evolution of the Byzantine Divine Liturgy', in Robert F. Taft, *Beyond East and West: Problems in Liturgical Understanding* (Washington, Pastoral Press, 1984), pp. 168ff.

2   Gregory Dix, *The Shape of the Liturgy* (London, Dacre, 1945), *passim*.

3   See discussion of this issue in Kenneth Stevenson, *The First Rites: Worship in the Early Church* (London, Marshall Pickering, 1989), pp. 4ff.

4   For a discussion of this issue, see my essay, 'The Eucharistic Prayer', in Michael Perham, ed., *Towards Liturgy 2000* (London, SPCK, 1989), pp. 48ff.

5   On the quaint evolution of this item, see Kenneth Stevenson, *Eucharist and Offering* (New York, Pueblo, 1986), pp. 149ff. It started as an offertory sentence in the Scottish 1637 rite, and ended as a full-blown prayer in the Scottish 1764 rite.

6   *Lutheran Book of Worship* (Minneapolis, Augsburg Publishing House, and Philadelphia, Board of Publication, Lutheran Church in America, 1978), p. 68.

7   Michael Ramsey, 'The Parish Communion', in *Durham Essays and Addresses* (London, SPCK, 1957), p. 18. The whole essay still speaks like a blueprint critique for much eucharistic faith and practice today.

8   *Patterns for Worship*, A Report by the Liturgical Commission of the General Synod of the Church of England, GS 898 (London, Church House Publishing, 1989), p. 237.

9   *The Book of Alternative Services of the Anglican Church of Canada* (Toronto, Anglican Book Centre, 1985), p. 214. This is also suggested in Kenneth Stevenson, *Accept This Offering: The Eucharist as Sacrifice Today* (London, SPCK, 1989), p. 82.

10 See *Patterns for Worship*, pp. 116ff. See also David Silk, *In Penitence and Faith: Texts for use with the Alternative Services* (London, Mowbray, 1988), pp. 10ff.

11 See the discussion in Stevenson, *Eucharist and Offering*, pp. 226ff.

12 *The Book of Common Prayer* (New York, Church Hymnal Corporation and Seabury Press, 1979), p. 361. A similar format is to be found in the Canadian *Book of Alternative Services*, where, however, there is scope for variable prayer, much of it fine, and general in scope.

13   Such a view was strongly taken by W. H. Frere, 'Climax and Anticlimax', in J. H. Arnold and E. G. P. Wyatt, *Walter Howard Frere: A Collection of his Papers on Liturgical and Historical Subjects*, Alcuin Club Collections 35 (London, Milford, 1940), p. 193. His stance is taken in the context of the kind of wider discussion of liturgical items we are advocating here.

14   Such a properly bound book of all the Gospels was similarly used in the nineteenth-century Catholic Apostolic ('Irvingite') rite.

5

Some Ecumenical Considerations

JOHN FENWICK

What constitutes specifically *Anglican* worship? The Liturgical Commission in *Patterns for Worship* suggests general characteristics,[1] but they are fairly minimalist and quite a number of other Churches would no doubt be happy with them as descriptions of the essential features of their own worship.

The same question could be asked of a whole range of Churches. What constitutes specifically Methodist, URC, Moravian or even Roman Catholic worship? The amount of cross-fertilization that has taken place between various Western Churches over the past three decades has blurred the distinction between their rites to a remarkable degree. The new URC Eucharist,[2] for example, is of general 'Hippolytan' shape and has the Roman offertory prayers ('Blessed are you . . .') and the Peace in the post-anaphoral position. There is very little about it that proclaims it exclusively as a rite of the Reformed tradition.

This is a phenomenon of considerable significance. It could be argued that what we have seen develop in recent years (at least as far as the Eucharist is concerned) is simply a single 'neo-Western rite' which happens to exist in a number of slightly different recensions. This has had a profound effect on ecumenical attitudes. Christians no longer emerge from attending each other's services saying, 'Gosh, wasn't it strange?', but, 'I'm amazed how like ours it was'. Once you realize that other Christians worship like you, then you begin to assume that they *are* very much like you and the barriers of prejudice and ignorance fall.

Undoubtedly the ASB 1980 has made a major contribution towards this largely healthy process. But what should ASB 2000 be doing? Now that we have discovered, almost by accident, that liturgical revision can contribute to ecumenism should we not undertake further revision with that aim more explicitly in view?

Space permits the exploration of only three areas.

(1) *Using the prayers of another tradition*

This, of course, has been happening for centuries. Cranmer clearly felt able simply to 'lift' the 'Prayer of St Chrysostom' from the Byzantine Eucharist and place it in his Daily Offices. Could something similar but perhaps more systematic not be done in the revision which lies ahead? Why should not ASB 2000 contain among its eucharistic prayers some of the classic anaphoras of Christian history? It would not prove too difficult to produce a suitably modified version of the anaphora of John Chrysostom, or St James, or even of the Roman Canon. (Something very similar could also be done with prayers from the initiation rites — or, indeed, from most other rites.) Some modification there would have to be, to cope with both genuine doctrinal difficulties and the need to harmonize with other rites, but to take such prayers into the Anglican treasury could be to enrich it immensely. Sensitively used and introduced they could enable Anglicans to identify with Churches and periods of church history which are currently beyond the awareness of many of them in anything but the vaguest sense.

Something along these lines has already been done in north America where a wide range of Churches agreed 'A Common Eucharist Prayer' based on the Egyptian recension of the anaphora of St Basil.[3] This prayer is thus found in the Prayer

Book of ECUSA and also forms the basis of Eucharistic Prayer IV of the revised Roman Mass. It is thus used in Anglican, Roman Catholic, Orthodox and Oriental Orthodox Churches and has some claim to be the most widely authorized anaphora in the Christian world. There would seem to be good reasons for authorizing its use in ASB 2000.

A similar argument could be made out for the Lima Liturgy which still crops up from time to time at ecumenical gatherings. If the Assembly of the WCC meeting in Canberra in February 1991 chooses to use it, that could well give it a new lease of life into the 1990s.

(2) Using the rites of the 'full communion' Churches

With a number of other Churches the Church of England has a relationship that is described as being in 'full communion'. The term is a rather imprecise one, but implies formal recognition of the other Church and of its ministry (all the Churches in this category possess bishops in the historic succession). Members of the Church of England may avail themselves of the ministrations of these Churches in the absence of their own (and vice versa) and in principle interchange of ministry is possible. (There are some limitations on this. At least four of the Churches in this category have women presbyters. Language can also impede free exchange. The clergy of these Churches may be granted an Archbishop's Licence to enable them to function in an Anglican context.)

The Churches themselves form an interesting group: the Lutheran Churches of Sweden (1909),[4] Finland (1930), Estonia (1938) and Latvia (1938); the Old Catholic Churches of the Union of Utrecht (1931); the Philippine Independent Church (1963); and the Mar Thoma Syrian Church (1974).

Liturgically, they present a fascinating range. Estonia and Latvia are 'primitive' German-style Lutheran. Sweden and Finland bear the marks of modern liturgical revision. The Old

Catholics, once staunch users of the Latin Mass, now possess a variety of rites (they are a family of independent Churches) often with Eastern features. The Philippine Church is quite Roman Catholic (of a rather old-fashioned form) in style; while the Mar Thoma Church stands unmistakably in the Syrian tradition with the full panoply of Orthodox worship. A rich feast — and all of it fully and legally available to Anglicans! Available, that is, under certain conditions. Those conditions can be quite restrictive. It would seem to be an anomaly that the status of being in full communion gives the Churches concerned no special privileges as far as the great bulk of Church of England Canon Law is concerned. In order to be designated under the Ecumenical Canons, for example, they have to go through the same process as a Church whose ministry we do not recognize and with which we are not in full communion. It is, arguably, areas like this which need further thought during the next phase of liturgical revision. Evolving worship should mean not simply writing yet more new texts but exploring more systematically the relationships we have with other Churches and their potential implications. The run-up to ASB 2000 should include discovering ways of making better use of the liturgical traditions that are already available to us.

(3) *The Ecumenical Canons*

Since the sixteenth century the main thrust of Anglican legislation relating to liturgy has been to *prevent* Anglican clergy from using anything other than the authorized rites — this is after all what Acts of Uniformity are all about. A sub-theme of this has been the attempt to ensure, not only that the authorized rites were used, but that they were used with specific ceremonial and ornaments. It was therefore very much the dawning of a new era when the Church of England promulgated a Canon permitting its clergy to take part in — and even preside at — services other than those of the Church of England.[5] Space does not permit a description and analysis of Canons B43 and B44 here. It is important to note, however, that they set up a new relationship between a presbyter and the liturgical traditions in which he operates. Most Anglican clergy have some experience of being 'dual-rite' (or even 'multi-rite'). They may preside at 1662 services in a particular church or at a particular time of day, and at ASB rites on other occasions. The new Canons extend this considerably. Under Canon B44.4 (1) (d) for example, it would be possible for a priest of the Church of England to preside regularly at, say, a Moravian Eucharist.[6] Presiding at worship is much more than simply 'taking a service'. It is about leading a group of people into the presence of God within a particular context, tradition, ethos and spirituality. To preside regularly at Moravian Eucharists should imply a willingness to enter into the heritage of that Church: its medieval origins, its missionary zeal, its particular expression of the relationship between the believer and Christ, and so on. To be prepared to do so could be a very exciting and enriching experience. Not to do so would reduce the permission given by the Canon to a mechanical function.

Thus the Ecumenical Canons, like the use of material from other rites and our relationships with the 'full communion' Churches, raise significant questions about liturgical identity, not simply for the Church of England as an institution, but for its clergy and people as the horizons of their experience of worship broaden. These are questions whose primary impact will not necessarily be on the *text* of ASB 2000 (though there must be some influence there), but on the climate of thought that will accompany its preparation and publication. Where might the process be leading? Just as it is possible to be a Roman Catholic of the Ukrainian rite or the Chaldean rite, might it be possible one day to be an Anglican of the Methodist or of the Syrian rite?

NOTES

1   GS 898 (London, Church House Publishing, 1989), p. 5.
2   *Service Book of the United Reformed Church*, Oxford, Clarendon Press, 1989.
3   See A. Houssiau, 'The Alexandrine Anaphora of St Basil', in L. Sheppard, ed., *The New Liturgy* (London, Darton Longman & Todd, 1970), pp. 228–43.
4   The dates in brackets are the year of the basic formal agreement of communion with the Church of England.
5   The Canons of course include provision for lay involvement as well.
6   The Moravian Church is one of the Churches designated by the Archbishops of Canterbury and York under the Church of England (Ecumenical Relations) Measure.

6

The Marriage Service

KENNETH STEVENSON

'Probably no service in the Prayer Book has undergone fewer changes since the Middle Ages than the Form for the Solemnization of Matrimony.'[1] So wrote Dean William Perry, one of the brains behind the Scottish Prayer Book of 1929, perhaps one of the most successful of revisions in the earlier part of this century.[2] Such an assertion is comforting and rewarding when we are looking for continuities in a world of change. We all know that the liturgy is at its most resistant to change on special occasions, and those special occasions are not just the solemn seasons of the liturgical year, they are also the solemn seasons of the human life-cycle. When people get married, it is asserted, they do not want a fresh liturgy each time.

And yet many pastors know full well that the contemporary marriage liturgy may be a very elaborate production, tailor-made to the couple. One thinks of the Royal Wedding of 1981, which bore the semblance of the Prayer Book form (which it followed for the first part) but which took on a much more complex use of liturgical material for its second part. One of the tools local clergy need above all else is a sort of anthology of material, a marital version of 'Funeral Services for the Christian Churches of England'.[3] It could contain the official texts of the mainstream Churches, together with a selection of readings and prayers. Such a publication would go a long way towards saving a great number of clergy a great deal of time.

This suggestion, which is offered in all seriousness, needs to be backed up by a more thorough revision of the ASB rite of Marriage. Dean Perry was right to suggest that the Prayer Book service was a conservative revision of the medieval rite. What we shall be arguing here is for that to be recognized, but to be recognized as inadequate for today's Church. ASB made several improvements of a notable sort, but it did not go far enough.

First of all, the ASB saw that the Prayer Book rite only made sense on its own terms when celebrated with a Eucharist. The couple are 'joined together' at the head of the nave, and then the priest walks with them up through a medieval chancel for the prayers at the Holy Table. But the Prayer Book was seldom, if ever, used with a Eucharist immediately following, and that made it end weakly; hence the various efforts to include a sermon and a blessing at the end. To meet that, ASB offers a service which can be combined more harmoniously with a Eucharist, or at least has a shape that closely resembles the first part of the Eucharist. Such a pattern is standard among the mainstream service books of today's West, including the Roman Catholic.[4]

But ASB did not finally resolve the dilemma, because the *shape* of the service can vary. This is a notable (and repeated) weakness in many of the other ASB services and it is the reason for so many of the varieties of shape discernible in, for example, the Eucharist. ASB likes variety of shape, which makes it difficult to use, whereas the American Episcopal Book of Common Prayer (1979)[5] opts at most stages for a uniform shape for most services, and this has the consequence of making it easier to use.

Thus, the ASB rite gives the Bible readings two main positions, either before the vows, or later on. It also allows the registration of the marriage to take place either half-way through or at the end, when it could have made the earlier position mandatory, thus providing the service with more coherence, so that the legal formalities set the seal on the vows (in legal terms) and it is the altar prayers (with or without the Eucharist) that give the climax to the rite. ASB was a compromise, and it would have been more successful had it made a firmer break with its great sixteenth-century predecessor. Uniformity of shape provides rhythm, too, for what is sometimes called an 'occasional office', and it also enables congregations to adapt to variety in the individual items themselves, e.g. readings and prayers, as people can adjust to them better if they always happen at the same place.

What shape, then, would be suggested? The one that lies behind the revisers' intentions in ASB, without the subsequent adjustments made in the interests of the Prayer Book tradition. This would result in the following shape:

> Introit and Exhortation
> Collect
> Readings
> Homily
> Consent
> Ring-giving
> Registration
> Prayers
> Blessing

Secondly, a revision of the ASB could, once such a shape is adopted as a groundplan, clothe it round with other items that illuminate what the whole rite is trying to say, in further adjustments, in new symbolism, and in more imaginative use of liturgical sources.

One of the adjustments that would heighten the dramatic focus of the service has already been pioneered in the American BCP (1979) over the way in which the consent is given. The Prayer Book, following the medieval English rites, in effect has *two* forms of consent: first a preliminary *question*, followed, secondly, by the active *vow*. (Other medieval rites handled the consent in different ways, and by no means all of them had the active vow, certainly not in the highly developed form of the fifteenth century.)[6]

BCP (1979) waxes yet more dramatic, for it separates the two forms of consent by placing the first (preliminary) after the opening exhortation, and putting the second (active vow) after the homily. The result is that both forms of consent are given a distinct role in the rite; the preliminary one gives the statement of intent, but the second (which is, in legal terms, the 'performative' one) comes only after the readings and homily. In other words the first part of the rite places a strong focus on the intention to marry, and the place of that intention within salvation history (the Bible read and preached in the face of this particular congregation).

The new symbolism[7] that could be introduced depends largely on local initiative and custom. When I was a parish priest in Lincolnshire it was not unknown for the groom to present the bride with precious coins after the exchange of rings. There are also other forms of symbolism which have been discussed at length elsewhere, such as the use of oil at the blessing of the couple (a Coptic custom that links marriage with initiation, and sees marriage as a vocation), the use of crowns (a practice universal in the East), or the use of a special canopy held over the couple during the blessing (a medieval procedure that survived the Lutheran Reformation in Sweden and is still an option today).

The most important symbolisms, however, are those which have a direct bearing on the congregation. There is no reason for the bride always to be 'given away' by a man, a medieval practice with feudal overtones. Each partner could be 'presented' for marriage by sponsors, thus making another kind of link with baptism. Candles are very popular in current practice and the 'wedding candle' is often a way of symbolizing the light of Christ shared by the two who become one flesh in marriage. But the restructuring of the rite along the lines suggested earlier, with the two forms of consent separated by the Word, would probably make the most profound symbolic point of all, for the couple would come forward first to say 'I will' and then have to return to their places before coming forward for the second (and final) time in order to make their solemn consent by reciting the vow.

More imaginative use of liturgical sources, too, might result in a rite that is at once enriched and clearer. The Prayer Book kept up the medieval fad for repeated blessings, and, indeed, the short blessings over the couple immediately before the nuptial Mass were a special feature of the medieval English marriage services. A revision of ASB could settle this matter once and for all by making a clearer distinction between two types of prayer 'over the couple' in the second part of the service. One would be a form of strong prayer, intercession for them. This could lead into a solemn blessing of the bridal pair, with the laying on of hands. Such a pattern is what appears in the BCP (1979), and, like most of its innovations, it has been taken over by other rites, not just Anglican ones. The intercession could, moreover, include themes that recur in the less happy experience of marriage that has been the twentieth century's experience. BCP (1979)'s text includes the following:

> Make their life together a sign of Christ's love to this sinful and broken world, that unity may overcome estrangement, forgiveness heal guilt, and joy conquer despair.[8]

The repertoire of medieval blessings is vast, but the following text, taken from the 1989 Liturgical Commission *Patterns for Worship* Report brings together a number of rich themes:

May God the Father join you together
in mutual love and faithful living,
as he united Adam and Eve, our first parents. Amen.

May the Lord Jesus be present with you
to bless your marriage with all his power
and gladden your hearts with the joy of Cana. Amen.

May the Holy Spirit fill you with a life of strength
and patience,
and crown you with the blessing of his heavenly gifts. Amen.
And the blessing . . .⁹

Thirdly, both the ASB and the Prayer Book rites have a
somewhat wooden expectation of participation, save in so far
as the couple themselves have to go through the ordeal of
reciting the vows. Participation is a slippery word, with even
more slippery meanings. Not everyone wants to recite things
aloud in public. And yet the ASB acclamations ('Blessed are
you, heavenly Father') strike a chord with many people, almost
as if the congregation finds its liturgical tongue for the first
time when these are recited, at the end of the first part of the
service. Once again, the BCP (1979) has led the way by
including a question to the congregation near the start of the
service, after the preliminary consent, as follows:

Will all of you witnessing these promises do all in your
power to uphold these two persons in their marriage?¹⁰

The reply is obvious and the meaning abundantly plain: and it
also spells out the fact that marriage is not just about two
people who happen to want each other, but is about the whole
of the community.

But another area of participation lies in the couple
themselves. Some modern Roman Catholic rites make provision
for the bridal pair to recite a prayer themselves, on their own

behalf, which would follow naturally from the vows. Just as the vow became a completely new kind of liturgical form and style, so such bridal prayers could develop their own shape and ambience. The Irish form includes the following formula, almost as a self-oblation:

You have given us to each other today.
Now together we give ourselves to you.[11]

Fourthly, the theology of the rite could do with adding two new nuances to its already full collation of ideas. One is the notion of marriage as *covenant*, which is a biblical theme and an approach to the theology of marriage that cuts across old battlegrounds of whether marriage is a sacrament or not. It also makes connections with baptism. To state in the opening exhortation that 'the bond and covenant of marriage was established by God in creation' also means that we see creation and redemption in one, and not divided by some special chasm. It also sets the scene for the vows soon to be made, as part of that ongoing covenant.

Another theological feature that could do with bringing out is in part a development of the previous one, to see the married couple as a kind of *'mini-church'*. In other words, marriage is an ecclesial ordinance, it is part of the Church, not a mere area of human relationships which the Church grudgingly recognizes. It is perhaps this latter aspect that will take a long time to enter into the consciousness of many people. The Eastern rites have long focused on the joy and celebration of marriage, as witness their love of using the miracle at Cana as the liturgical reading, whereas the most common nuptial mass lesson in the Middle Ages was Jesus pronouncing on indissolubility. Both are, of course, necessary, and yet one senses that the Western religious tradition as it has been inherited (and not necessarily how it was originally worked out!) is somewhat negative and defensive.

Fifthly, and finally, all of this needs to be set within a much wider framework. In 1909, the French social anthropologist Arnold Van Gennep wrote his pioneering work, *The Rites of Passage,*[12] in which he drew attention to three phases through which people go when they experience a significant change. First there is a rite of separation, in the course of which the individual or group is marked off for future change. Then there is the phase of 'liminality', in which the individual or group undergoes a trying time of living on the edge — it is a time of preparation. Finally, there is the rite of incorporation, in which the individual or group celebrates its new status, which is recognized by the community.

The parallel between this series and Christian initiation in its primitive and 'adult' form is plain for all to see. The catechumen enrols — and is 'separated' from the congregation. This becomes the period of the catechumenate, living 'on the edge', not yet being able to receive communion, standing in a special place in church. The whole series comes to a glorious climax in the baptismal Eucharist. That is the incorporation *par excellence.*

The question is, can this scheme have anything to say about marriage? The Bible is full of examples of betrothal preceding marriage, not least in the story of Mary and Joseph, where (as is made clear) the betrothal was legally binding, although Joseph could have set aside the contract if Mary was pregnant by another man. The early evidence and subsequent liturgies point to a similar scheme for celebrating marriage, and these are still to be found throughout the East, although in practice the rites are usually celebrated together, or on the same day. For betrothal is a public rite, whose original purpose was to earmark the couple's intention to marry in the future. There would then be a time of engagement, in the course of which the community would pray for them, and prepare for the marriage themselves. Finally, the marriage celebration would be a liturgy in its own rite, closely resembling the first part of the Eucharist, and in some cases leading directly into it.

Current work by Roman Catholics in this country indicates that they are taking seriously this aspect of history and are making bold attempts to reclaim it for themselves, not as a piece of false primitivism, but as a way of celebrating marriage in a world in which marriage itself needs as much strengthening as the Church can give it. A 'phased' rite would be an option, and one where the couple ritualize publicly their engagement, after which the local congregation prays for them (the banns of marriage made sense?!), all of which finally leads into the marriage service itself.

Such a format has the advantage of spreading the sacrament of marriage over a far wider terrain than it has occupied for many centuries. It could demarginalize our marital practice and rescue it from trivialization. Such attention to what are often called liturgy's 'deep structures' (the things that lie below the surface no matter what later history does to them) may well be the path of the future Church. A revision of ASB should include something along these lines. It could prove pastorally desirable and liturgically enriching.

A friend recently wrote to me after looking after a group of parishes in the north for a few weeks. Having spent most of his ministry in non-parochial work, he was naturally looking forward to encountering the scene at what is sometimes referred to as 'the coal-face' of the Church. In the course of those few weeks, he had to preside over three weddings, and he was appalled at the way things had changed. Being prone to slight exaggeration, he described the service as 'a more or less equal mixture of the Chelsea Flower Show, Trooping the Colour, the Miss World Competition, and a Film Company on location'. Behind the cant of that description there lies more than a grain of truth. And there is little that new rites can do if one sees them primarily as doing battle with modern culture.

At the end of the day, every parish priest will have to make a decision about many matters that are far higher on couples' agendas than which readings to have, and whether to include some new symbolism. But I wonder if the current fad for going over the top at weddings is not really in part a commentary on the rather dismal liturgies that we have used at marriages for some time.

Each of the areas which I have suggested for further exploration could serve a revision of ASB — and thousands of couples — well in the future. Perhaps most basic of all is the last suggestion of all: that we need to 'phase' marriage, if only to get across to people that what they do anyway (most relationships are phased) has a public and ecclesial counterpart. Such a pattern may well engender more realism about marriage, in its light and shade, joy and sorrow, pain and possibility. Liturgy, after all, is there to serve God and his people — not the other way round.

NOTES

1   W. Perry, *The Scottish Prayer Book — Its Value and History* (Cambridge, University Press, 1929), p. 117.
2   See Kenneth Stevenson, *Nuptial Blessing: A Study of Christian Marriage Rites*, Alcuin Club Collections 64 (London, SPCK, 1982), pp. 181ff.
3   *Funeral Services of the Christian Churches in England*, Norwich, The Canterbury Press, 1986, by the Joint Group on Funeral Services at Cemeteries and Crematoria.
4   See Kenneth Stevenson, *To Join Together: The Rite of Marriage*, Studies in the Reformed Rites of the Catholic Church, vol. v (New York, Pueblo, 1987), pp. 113ff., and *passim*.
5   *The Book of Common Prayer* (New York, Church Hymnal Corporation and The Seabury Press, 1979), pp. 423ff.
6   See Stevenson, *Nuptial Blessing*, pp. 68ff.
7   See Stevenson, *To Join Together*, pp. 194ff.

8 See *The Book of Common Prayer*, p. 429.
9 *Patterns for Worship*, A Report by the Liturgical Commission of the General Synod of the Church of England, GS 898 (London, Church House Publishing, 1989), p. 262.
10 See *The Book of Common Prayer*, p. 425.
11 Quoted in Stevenson, *To Join Together*, p. 160.
12 This is the backbone of the thinking behind Stevenson, *To Join Together*, and is discussed in detail from pp. 7ff.

7

Healing and Reconciliation

PAUL ROBERTS

I

The last liturgies of healing to be considered by the Church of England led to the authorization of *Ministry to the Sick*[1] in 1983. During the process additional material for the Reconciliation of a Penitent[2] failed to win the necessary synodical approval, and has never been authorized. Time is now due for a reassessment of the liturgical provision which exists in the Church of England for ministry falling within the domain of 'healing'. 'Reconciliation' has inevitably been linked to healing through the association present in the provisions of the 1662 BCP, although each subject covers areas which the other does not.

The provision of the 1662 BCP has never been popular,[3] partly because of its suggestion that the sickness is a result of the person's sin, but mainly because ministry to the sick requires more flexibility than a set format usually allows. *Ministry to the Sick* moved the emphasis from exclusively the home towards services in a wider range of contexts — home, hospital or parish church. The implied connection with personal sin is gone, and the services allow for great flexibility, recognizing the constraints which hospital, home or sickness may apply. Yet the fact of material having gone through the detailed process of full synodical revision raises the question as to whether it has got *too much* authority attached to it. The inadequacy of the BCP services led to a large number of suggestions for more practical services, and a tradition of flexibility and innovation has always existed in this area, closely linked to the variation in pastoral practice down the centuries. It seems unnecessary, and pastorally misguided, to insist that all services produced by the Church which focus upon healing should have to be subjected to full synodical processes. Is this not a case of the Worship and Doctrine Measure being too literally followed? [4]

II

It is this tradition of innovation which may hold the key to future liturgical provision in the area of healing. The ethos of services for healing has been greatly expanded in recent decades. Whereas the early twentieth century saw provision for services pioneered by groups with a distinctly Catholic emphasis, the healing service continues to expand in use across church traditions. Evangelicals, though originally antipathetic to healing services, and anointing especially, came to see the need for some liturgical provision for healing ministry. Most significantly, the Charismatic Renewal's emphasis on the action of God through the gifts of members of the Body of Christ has spilled over into the domain of healing ministry. In the last ten years, a large number of titles from the range of traditions has been published, and the subject continues to enjoy a large and wide readership. Perhaps as a result of this, there are most welcome signs of much cross-fertilization and consultation.

At the same time, the sheer range of 'methodology' leads to a corresponding range of liturgical expression. If the Church is to respond to this with authorized forms, then it is tempting to say that it will have to be prepared to produce material which is either extremely comprehensive, or so general as to be of questionable value in any particular situation. Any future provision will need to address at least as much effort to accompanying notes dealing with the application of the material as to any suggested material itself. If the case for this approach can be made for normal Sunday worship (as, for example, in *Patterns for Worship*),[5] so much the more for liturgical provision for healing ministry.

When *Ministry to the Sick* was produced, the Charismatic and Evangelical traditions in the Church were only just beginning to make a mark on liturgy for healing. If numbers and sales of publications are an index, this situation has now radically altered. Similarly, further developments of specialized approaches in Christian healing need to be taken into account, as they raise specific issues which any healing liturgy needs to address. It is to these issues that we now turn.

Firstly, what is the place of the non-ordained? In the 1983 services the presidency of the rite and the administration of anointing can be performed only by a priest, while the laying on of hands can be delegated only to an 'authorized lay minister'. This is to envisage too narrow a range of liturgical settings, and encourages the view that prayer for healing is a matter for the 'specialists'.[6] For example, many churches now practise regular laying on of hands in the course of a communion service, often held in a side chapel or a secluded part of the church, while the priest is occupied with the administration of communion. The parish priest needs the liturgical flexibility to delegate to sensitive and gifted non-ordained, and to be free to choose the contexts and occasions most suited to the exercise of this ministry. Many clergy will testify to the way gifts of healing have been discovered in the congregation, yet the liturgy's use of ministers needs to encourage all the congregation to discover their gifts.

Secondly, what of the desire for the supernatural? One of the recent approaches to healing which has achieved great popularity lays emphasis upon the expectation of miracle, speaking in terms of 'paradigm shift' from the ordinary to the supernatural.[7] The majority of those involved in healing ministry would not wish to exclude miraculous healing, but may question whether this generates an unnecessary dualism between healing through scientific and 'supra-scientific' processes. In terms of liturgy, this question is focused upon the interaction between the words and actions of the liturgy, and the expectations they reflect and affect. Questions of emphasis should be asked: How much does the rite speak of healing through medical means? Is God seen as one who aids or intervenes? Are we praying for a miracle or for help? Within each approach ritual actions have developed which reflect where the emphasis lies, and official suggestions cannot but address the issue. The middle course may or may not be the right one. Here again, pastoral commentary and flexibility are much needed.

Thirdly, we need to look at healing as a 'commodity'. Liturgies of healing need to address the relationship between our cultural approach to health and sickness, and our theology of the Church's ministry of healing. The attitudes and expectations which people bring to a service of healing are shaped by societal norms, in particular questions of the rights of an individual to a good life, and the assumptions about illness arising from a relatively advanced medical system. Here the work of comparative liturgy can provide insights across cultures and history which will be of benefit to the pastoral theologian as well as to the Liturgical Commission. Is the Church inevitably pushed into the realm of the 'last resort' when medical treatment fails? Or does this in turn lead to the Church seeing itself more in terms of 'alternative medicine'? The increasing popularity of a holistic approach to medicine indicates that the cultural issues are being discussed beyond the official bounds of the Church. An interesting comment upon this is that in certain areas of South America it is common to pray over an aspirin tablet before taking it because its cost is high and the expectation of its working by no means certain.[8]

III

We turn now to the ministry of reconciliation. The failure to get synodical approval for the material for the Reconciliation of a Penitent centred upon Evangelical misgivings over the formula, 'I absolve you from all your sins'. This issue dominated the debate to such a degree that other issues, such as the desirability and necessity of such material in the wider context of sin and reconciliation, were largely overlooked. The appearance of John Macquarrie's paper on the subject[9] suffered a poor reception by Synod largely because it failed to take into account the way the discussion had centred around a single issue in what is a very large area. The appearance of a very brief form in *Lent, Holy Week, Easter* which uses the phrase 'I declare that you are absolved from all your sins' has the marks of a Commission desiring to pour oil on troubled waters by using a formula which will not arouse adversaries, while giving some provision vaguely related to the origin of the offending material. In practice, lacking as it does any explanatory notes, it amounts to bad practice on the part of the Commission and an example of a liturgically diplomatic fudge, which is of questionable use and which is possibly misleading. There are, after all, serious issues concerning the reconciliation of penitents which still have not been faced.

In the last decade a considerable amount of research into the liturgical origins of reconciliation has taken place.[10] Reviewing the debate of the early 1980s one gets the impression that the outlook of both sides had progressed little beyond those of the late medieval period. Future debate would benefit from the recognition that '*Ego te absolvo*' does not mark the zenith or *sine qua non* of universal church practice in reconciliation, but that the Church has always had, and still has, a diversity of practice in regard to the appropriate form and context for reconciliation of penitents. '*Ego te absolvo*' is a shibboleth which should be dropped by both sides.

Consideration needs to be given to the way this plurality of practice has existed within the Anglican Communion itself. The relative merits of the Reformation stress on general confession and absolution, private confession and absolution, and personal confession to God are due for reconsideration in the Anglican context as much as they are being reconsidered in contemporary Catholicism.[11] The overemphasis upon the issues surrounding auricular confession and absolution betrays a view of sin and holiness which is too narrow, ignoring as it does the societal impact of sin. Those who hear confessions regularly testify to the limited field of concerns surrounding the ministry, or the difficulties in handling the complexity of sin in modern society where a diversity of ethic permeates as far as the Church itself.[12]

Such reconsiderations would be liturgical as much as they would be theological and ethical. There is need for a reassessment of the place of confession in contexts broader than the formal and traditional. For example, confession and absolution often happen in healing services as part of the ministry, often lay-administered, happening quite unself-consciously.

Coherent liturgical expression of the ministry of reconciliation will only arrive after detailed consideration of what sin and holiness are. If sin is examined in all its social, theological and personal spheres ('We have sinned against you, ourselves and our neighbours . . .') then a clearer understanding of what absolution is will emerge. Again, if holiness (social, theological and personal) is clearly placed once again on the agenda of the Church, the meaning of penance and the importance of confession will gain a new liturgical significance. However, this is by no means simple. The continuing debate within the Church over issues of sexuality illustrates the problems of proclaiming standards of holiness amid uncertainty over what is sin, and how to deal with it in the public life of the Church. It is poor solace to remember that these issues stem from the earliest origins of the rite of penance, yet the history suggests that discussions concerning sin and holiness benefit, and are benefited by, discussions of ecclesiology. Enormous issues though these are, the pastoral and spiritual health of the Church will only be served by effort expended in grappling with them, rather than by brushing the whole lot under the carpet.

The liturgists can make an important contribution by drawing upon the strong ecumenical links within their discipline. As has been mentioned, within Roman Catholicism there is much discussion about the emerging pattern of reconciliation since the arrival of the revised rites. This suggests parallel problems of privatized views of sin and forgiveness, unease over the role of the priest in absolution and difficulties in finding a rationale for confession because of confusion over holiness. Again the picture is familiar. It is as though the Church already has the vaccine, in the forgiveness of sins proclaimed in the Gospel, but is confused over the precise method of administration, and the conditions for which it is required. An agreed code of practice is still a long way off.

NOTES

1   CUP, Clowes, Mowbray, OUP and SPCK, 1983.
2   The Commission's report was published in *The Blessing of Oils and the Reconciliation of a Penitent*, GS 472, London, CIO, 1980. The Revision Committee's Text was subsequently published in *The*

Form for the Reconciliation of a Penitent, GS 530, London, Church House Publishing, n.d.

3 G. J. Cuming, *A History of Anglican Liturgy* (2nd edn, London, Macmillan, 1982), pp. 135, 173.

4 Arguably, only services for the 'Visitation of the Sick' and 'Communion of the Sick' (in the house) can be strictly regarded as alternative to the BCP, and therefore all other proposals could be 'commended' by the House of Bishops. However, the appearance of *Ministry to the Sick* may have set a restrictive precedent.

5 *Patterns for Worship*, A Report by the Liturgical Commission of the General Synod of the Church of England, GS 898, London, Church House Publishing, 1989; at the time of writing, these proposals are about to go to initial consideration by Synod.

6 Canon B37, referred to by the notes to the service, mentions only the visitation of a sick person at home, not healing services held in the parish church. Furthermore, who are the 'lawful ministers' referred to by the notes for which no provision exists in canon?

7 The approach has been popularized by the writings of John Wimber, for example his *Power Healing*, London, Hodder & Stoughton, 1986, and has been emulated in parish models in this country.

8 This provides a vivid echo of the origins of anointing with blessed oil.

9 *The Reconciliation of a Penitent*, A Report by Professor John Macquarrie, GS Misc 258, London, Central Board of Finance of the Church of England, 1987.

10 This has been helpfully summarized in a series of articles arising from the Brixen conference of *Societas Liturgica*, which have been published in *Studia Liturgica* 18.1, 1988.

11 e.g. Robert C. Garafalo, 'Reconciliation and Celebration: A Pastoral Case for General Absolution', *Worship* 63.5, 1989.

12 See Perry Butler, 'Introduction: Confession Today', in M. Dudley and G. Rowell, ed., *Confession and Absolution*, London, SPCK, 1990.

8

Confirmation and its Future

DAVID STANCLIFFE

I

In 1932 Bishop Hensley Henson, that fierce defender of traditional Anglicanism, conducted a survey among his brother bishops to see whether they were adhering to the canonical minimum age for confirmation — fourteen. They were not; and he wrote gloomily to the Bishop of Exeter about what he believed to be this recklessly romanizing trend. He could see where it would end; what would stop them from confirming at twelve, or ten, or even seven? Once on that path, would it not be as entirely logical 'if, with the easterns, we blessed oil in central cauldrons and authorised the parish priests to apply it to the regenerated babes'?[1] At least, such a practice would have the benefit of removing the excuse for proposals to divide the historic dioceses, against which he was waging another of his crusades.

What would he have made of today's debates about the place of confirmation in relation to baptism, to admission to communion, to adult affirmation, and to empowering for service in the royal priesthood of the whole company of Christian people? Above all, what is its place in relation to the person of the bishop, who, in the Anglican tradition alone, is still the only authorized minister of the rite?

The traditional answer to these questions has been to say that confirmation in some way completes baptism and is

71

therefore a prerequisite for admission to holy communion. Furthermore, this 'completion' is only on offer to those who can affirm for themselves the promises made on their behalf at their baptism. In other words, confirmation has to be earned by intellectual assent, and without it you are no more than a Victorian child, brought down to the drawing room for half an hour after tea in the nursery! But this view is under serious pressure.

In the first place, there is broad ecumenical consensus[2] that baptism, the sacrament of initiation into the life of Christ, properly leads directly to the Eucharist, the sacrament of abiding and growing in that life. St Paul is very clear that anyone who is baptized, who is one with Christ in his death and in his resurrection, is a member of the Body of Christ. Theologically, this must be so. It is impossible to conceive how one could be only partly 'in Christ': either you are or you aren't. Admission to communion, therefore, must follow baptism.

While the logic of this position has always been recognized, and indeed practised in varying ways in Churches as diverse as the Roman Catholic Church and the United Reformed Church, it has not been easy to see a way out of the peculiarly Anglican practice of baptism, then a gap, then confirmation, and only then communion — a pattern recognized as 'intolerable' as long ago as 1927 by Oliver Quick.[3] Behind the traditional position lurked the belief that while baptism signalled rebirth and the forgiveness of sins, it was confirmation which conveyed the grace of the Spirit, and so was necessary to complete the rite of initiation. One solution was to propose the restoration of the (supposed) primitive unity between baptism, confirmation and the Eucharist, emphasizing the essentially adult nature of the rite. This patristic model, vigorously championed by Dom Gregory Dix and deriving heavily from Cyril of Jerusalem as a fourth-century golden norm, has dominated discussion of initiation over the last twenty years. The norm for initiation rites in the ASB is a service of Baptism, Confirmation and Holy Communion for adults, and services such as Baptism of Infants and Confirmation on its own are derived from this unitive model.

Predictably, one of the consequences of this has been the attempt to move away from infant baptism as the norm, a shift which the more committed churchgoer found it easier to understand than the less regular attender. Alongside this has grown an understanding of the Church as the Body of Christ, the company of the faithful, which has emphasized sharper boundaries between the insiders and the irregulars, and has led to the charge that the Church of England is moving rapidly from being the national church into becoming a eucharistic sect. But to lay the responsibility for this perceptible shift exclusively at the door of a theology of initiation adopted during the 1960s would be too simplistic; many other factors have been at work.

For example, a large number of Anglicans have been brought up on a model of infant baptism and teenage instruction concluded by confirmation, leading to more or less regular communicant status. Infant baptism was the expected norm, whether or not parents were churchgoers, and was available more or less on demand. Teenage confirmation classes with a carrot-like service of confirmation as the climax were a rite of passage from childhood into adulthood: in confirmation you made your baptism your own. This pattern, relying heavily on the candidate's own decision (or sometimes on the wishes of the parents), has not been entirely superseded by the ASB norm.

But there is a third model. Here, childhood initiation, probably through infant baptism (and quite possibly teenage confirmation), is followed by a period of lapsing or merely routine observance from which there is an awakening or renewal, and the need to celebrate coming to full faith. One result of this tendency is that the demand for adult baptism has increased very considerably. But, perhaps of more significance, there is also the demand for 're-baptism' — for a more significant and memorable act than that sprinkling of an infant from a bird-bath or even ash-tray font which goes by the popular name of christening.

Behind this longing for a more dramatic and significant rite lies the genuine desire to express in the moment of initiation something of our union with the death and resurrection of Christ. For those who have come to full faith after a period of darkness, this, and not an unremembered infant christening, is the moment when the language of St Paul (Rom. 6.3–11) — being buried with Christ by baptism into death — seems most real.

This feeling is powerfully reinforced by the texts in the ASB, which concentrate almost exclusively on the paschal character of baptism, on the link in baptism between the death and resurrection of Christ and the dying and rising of the believer as he goes down into the deep waters of death. But there is another strand in the theology and practice of baptism which balances the anamnesis of Christ's death and resurrection with a strong emphasis on the new birth by water and the epiclesis of the Spirit (John 3). In this tradition, the pattern of Jesus' own baptism as the inauguration of his conscious sonship is what is embraced in the rite. The imagery of the new creation, of baptism as an epiclesis of the Spirit, predominates, and the proper dominance of Easter is balanced by Epiphany.

A baptism rite, or at least a baptismal prayer over the water, that has some reference to this tradition[5] might do a lot to free the celebration of baptism in the ASB from its strait-jacket, and by reintroducing rebirth as a key concept, help to keep in play a valuable insight in the historic Anglican tradition of infant baptism. Inevitably, a baptismal practice that has centred almost exclusively on the Romans 6 model encourages a 'moment' theology, a sharp line between death and resurrection, between pre- and post- conversion, between before and after baptism. That kind of baptismal theology makes for a Church that is very hard at the edges and in which the concept of gradual coming to faith is more difficult to embrace. Yet it is just that gradual coming to faith to which the Catechumenate Movement seeks to respond, and which was discovered to be the preferred path of the majority of those who responded by sustained inquiry to the last Billy Graham mission in London. That is why the Church needs to make room for a pattern of initiation which allows for, and even expects, staged rites.

But by staged rites, do I mean a rite of infant baptism which marks a new birth by water, and leaves the Spirit to be given by a later act of confirmation? The answer is, No. Integral to such 'staged rites' is a sense of the powerful and pervasive presence of the Spirit in awakening repentance and turning before baptism as much as in baptism itself, and in the confirmation and empowering for ministry which may follow. It is this theological perception, that baptism is our personal Pentecost in fulfilment of Joel's prophecy (2.28–9), that has united with liturgical scholarship to make it well-nigh impossible to believe that confirmation adds some special ingredient to what was given in water baptism, in other words, that baptism is only the entry into the dying and rising of Christ, which confirmation completes in the outpouring of the Spirit, much as Pentecost in Luke/Acts completes Easter.

II

Given an initiation rite which allows a sense of staged growth under the formative guidance of the Holy Spirit, what then are we to make of confirmation? A good deal of research has taken place in recent years on the nature of post-baptismal anointing in the Syriac–Armenian rite.[6] There we learn that the Pauline imagery of Romans 6 was not always so central as it is today. 'In the oldest Syriac and Armenian sources Christian baptism is modelled on Jesus' baptism in the Jordan, interpreted as the Messianic anointing of Jesus (Lk 4.18; Acts 10.38), an anointing into the Messianic priesthood of Christ that the Christian too receives.'[7] In this tradition, the key text is not Romans 6, but John 3; the climax is not the water bath, but the anointing; and the font is not just a tomb, but a womb.

There are also hints that the function of bishops in confirmation was not to impose a second anointing, but rather to recognize and to ratify the status of the newly baptized by laying hands on them. 'Confirmation was adopted for reasons strictly juridical in nature, not as a result of theological reflection on the essence of the rite.'[8]

As the principal minister of the rite of Christian initiation, the bishop will whenever possible preside over baptism. Winkler points out the importance of it being the same minister who presides over both baptism and chrismation, and this is reinforced by the decision of the Roman Catholic bishops in the USA which declares that those baptizing priests who have the right to administer confirmation *must* exercise it; the bishop cannot prohibit them. What then is the distinctive role of the bishop? 'We can naturally only welcome the fact that in many places in America a meeting with the bishop, who has delegated to priests baptism and confirmation at the Easter vigil, takes place at Pentecost . . .'[9] In this legislation for the contemporary Roman Catholic Church we can see the seeds of the confusion which has bedevilled discussion about initiation for generations. For what is here being called 'confirmation' is what Winkler (and the Eastern Church) calls chrismation, that anointing which is the powerful counterpart to the water baptism, and rightly belongs integrally with it. But it is not what Winkler has identified as confirmation in south Gaul, nor what Aidan Kavanagh believes it to be — a distinctively episcopal rite.

Kavanagh argues[10] that confirmation is distinct from the post-baptismal chrismation, and is a 'Missa', a rite of hand-laying that originally had its own pattern of readings and prayers, and marked the moment of transition between the baptismal and the eucharistic rites. Such hand-layings were a distinctively episcopal feature and formed a significant part in the celebration of the office at Jerusalem, according to Egeria, who describes the amount of time that the bishop gave to these personal blessings, as he sent the faithful on their way. I have witnessed something similar in the Orthodox Liturgy: it was attended, though not celebrated, by the bishop for the first time in weeks; and throughout there was a constant stream of people 'coming to his hand' for a personal blessing. Such a practice is attested in the *Apostolic Constitutions*, where the liturgical structure of confirmation is like any other: a petitionary blessing prayer, said by the bishop, followed by a 'coming to his hand' by those he has blessed. Confirmation does not take the place of chrismation; it is a solemn ratification of a completed initiation into the assembly.

III

But such historical considerations are of more than academic interest to us only if they look like illuminating the pastoral and ecclesial questions we have to solve now. Do they help us make sense of confirmation in relation to baptism, belonging and the Eucharist in the Church of England now?

I believe they do. First, they allow us to see that baptism is a pneumatically complete rite of initiation in itself, an initiation into the risen life of Christ by water and the Spirit. Secondly, they underline a continuing distinct function for confirmation — not as a rite of admission to holy communion, nor as the

passing of a test in intellectual or spiritual maturity —
justification by knowledge or worthiness! — but as a rite of
association with the bishop.

This persistent connection between confirmation and the
bishop has led some[11] to attach a theological rationale — the
giving of the Holy Spirit — to a rite which originally had a
simply structural ancestry. If we reject this imposed rationale,
what sense are we to make of 'Coming to the bishop's hand for
a Missa'? Most people recognize the bishop's hand-laying as
the formal liturgical act; but the moment they remember is
the bishop's farewell at the church door — taking them by the
hand, looking them in the eye and challenging them to live
the life of the gospel. This personal, one-to-one sending out
on the way reflects more of the feeling of the bishop's 'Missa'.

I am not suggesting that the administration of confirmation
be reduced to bishops standing around in porches. What I do
suggest is that we begin to think of confirmation more in
terms of a ratification of what was instituted fully in baptism,
an extended and strengthened incorporation into the conscious
life of the Church and its responsibilities, and an authoritative
sending out for ministry. Confirmation would 'complete'
baptism in much the same sense that the prayer, 'Send us out
in the power of your Spirit . . .', with the subsequent blessing
and dismissal may be said to complete the Eucharist.
Confirmation would then be seen less as part of the rite of
initiation and more by analogy with other distinctively episcopal
rites such as ordination. It is a rite which gives pattern and
direction to the life of the Body of Christ, pointing its members
in the direction in which their gifts lie, and conferring Christ's
authority for their use in the service of his Kingdom.

Thinking like this underlies the treatment of confirmation
in the 1979 Book of Common Prayer of ECUSA, where
confirmation is grouped not with services of baptism and
reconciliation, but with episcopal offices. It is linked with

reception and reaffirmation, and is clearly focused on ecclesial identity. There is a presentation and examination, but the Apostles' Creed is rehearsed by the Church as a whole, and not just by the candidates 'to see if we are getting it right or not'. And the Apostles' Creed is filled out by an apostolic charge:

'Will you continue in the Apostles' teaching and fellowship . . .?'

There is no renewal of the chrismation with which the baptismal rite concluded when the prayer was that 'all who are sealed with this Chrism may share in the royal priesthood of Jesus Christ'.

The Bishop's prayer for the 'candidates' in confirmation makes reference to the sealing of the Spirit decisively in the past tense and prays, not for a further dose of the Spirit, but for renewal in the existing Covenant:

' . . . by the sealing of your Holy Spirit,
you have bound us in your service;
renew in these the Covenant . . .'

The prayer then moves to words close to those in the Dismissal Prayer in the Eucharist:

'Send them forth in the power of the Holy Spirit'

and these words are echoed in what the bishop says to each as he lays his hands on them:

'Strengthen, O Lord, your servant N with your Holy Spirit,
empower him for your service;
and sustain him . . .'

Confirmation is a ratification of baptism, the public recognition of those messianic gifts and an empowering for active and conscious service.

What would a revision of baptism and confirmation along

these lines offer to the Church of England today?

First, such a revision would put an end, once and for all, to thinking of confirmation as the pneumatic completion of baptism, by providing a full and unitive rite of initiation consisting of renunciation, water baptism and the seal of the Spirit along the model of Christ's baptism. This pneumatically strong and unitive baptismal rite would be especially welcome ecumenically.

Second, it would put an end to the agonized debate as to whether baptism is sufficient basis for admission to communion or not, and would allow the 'Children in the Way' debate to take place on its own terms, and for confirmation to be released from its function as a turnstile to communion.

Third, it would retain a decisively episcopal rite of confirmation, which would find its place along with ordination and commissioning for particular ministries among the episcopal offices, rather than as part of the rite of initiation. Indeed, the one gesture of hand-laying would need to be accompanied by variable formulae for a number of different occasions. Confirmation in these terms would be much more akin to what, for example, a Methodist — or even a Roman Catholic — who had become a regular communicant in the Church of England might experience, in deciding to seek formal admission to and put his gifts at the disposal of the life of his local parish.

Fourth, confirmation has had a varied history, and different ages have slanted it in their own way. There now seems to be both liturgical and ecumenical convergence on an understanding of confirmation which has to do with affirming our baptism, making public a commitment to the life of the Church and having the gifts we offer in the service of the Kingdom recognized by the Church's principal minister.

NOTES

1 Hensley Henson to the Bishop of Exeter on 10 January 1933, in *Selected Letters*, ed. Brayley, London, SPCK, 1950.

2 *Baptism, Eucharist and Ministry* (The Lima Text), Geneva, World Council of Churches, 1982; see especially the Commentary on The Eucharist, section 19.

3 O. C. Quick, *The Christian Sacraments* (London, Nisbett, 1927), pp. 182, 184.

4 Dom Gregory Dix, *The Theology of Confirmation in relation to Baptism* (Westminster, Dacre, 1945), pp. 34-5.

5 See, for example, the prayers over the water in the Service for The Feast of the Baptism of the Lord in the report edition of *The Promise of his Glory*, London, Church House Publishing, 1990.

6 Gabriele Winkler, 'Confirmation or Chrismation? A Study in Comparative Liturgy', *Worship* 58.1 (1984), pp. 2-17.

7 Robert Taft, reviewing G. Winkler, *Das armenische Initiationsrituale*, Rome, Pontificium Institutum Studiorum Orientalium, 1982, in *Worship* 58.3 (1984), pp. 264-6.

8 Gabriele Winkler, op. cit., p. 16.

9 Balthasar Fischer, 'The National Statutes for the Catechumenate approved by the Conference of Bishops of the USA on November 11, 1986', *Studia Liturgica* 19.2 (1989), pp. 129-30.

10 Aidan Kavanagh, 'Confirmation: A Suggestion from Structure', *Worship* 58.5 (1984), pp. 386-95.

11 For example, J. P. C. Fisher, *Confirmation Then and Now*, Alcuin Club Collections 60, London, SPCK, 1978.

9

Ordination

BRYAN SPINKS

A preliminary question to be addressed on the services of ordination is whether or not the Ordinal should even be included in the revision of a prayer book for 2000. Historically the rites of ordination were in the Pontifical, the bishop's book, because these rites were regarded as his domain, and he could and did make his own additions and emendations to the rites. The first Anglican Ordinal of 1550 was quite separate from the Prayer Book of 1549, and even when it was included in the 1552 Prayer Book, it retained its separate title. It is perhaps not without significance that the ordination rites of the ASB were never published separately, but circulated in draft form until the appearance of the 1980 book — suggesting that general access to these services was not too important. Some have felt that the ASB is already overloaded, and the book for 2000 could be slimmed down by omitting material such as the ordination rites.

The omission of the ordination rites would, I think, be a regrettable step, and would reinforce the opinion held by some layfolk that the services are not really their business, but only concern those few who become deacons and priests, and the even fewer who are selected to be bishops. The Ordinal has a crucial doctrinal position in the Anglican Church, being a sign of our intention to be part of the Church universal — a concern enshrined in the Chicago–Lambeth Quadrilateral. It is an important part of our ecclesiology, and for this reason needs to be retained as part of the 'common prayer' of the Church of England.

There is perhaps also a case for making its position in such a book more prominent. All Christians have a ministry, since all are made members of the royal priesthood through baptism. It is through baptism into the *ecclesia* that all ministry derives, since we are in Christ. Within the royal priesthood there are distinctive ministries, and in the past a number of ministries have been singled out for liturgical recognition.[1] The distinctive ministries of bishop, presbyter and deacon cannot be entirely separated from other gifts, charisms and offices, since they all stem from baptism. Possibly the ordination services should be placed after baptism, with confirmation removed (as in the American Prayer Book) to the 'Pastoral offices'. This would at least make the point that all Christians have ministry through baptism, and the distinctive ministries derive from the general ministry of the royal priesthood.

The ordination rites of the ASB can trace their pedigree back to the recommendation of E. C. Ratcliff for the Anglican–Methodist Ordinal. A major concern of those rites was stated quite clearly by Ratcliff when he wrote to the chairman of the Anglican–Methodist Ordinal Sub-Committee: 'Now is the time to finish with Anglican forms and their mistakes, and to turn to simpler and older patterns which are clear as to meaning and not open to objections on the ground of "prelacy".'[2]

This concern was followed in the ASB by making clear that ordination was by prayer and the laying on of hands, and has nothing to do with formulae or insignia. Here the ASB forms are from a theological point of view admirable, and in no need of any fundamental revision.

Having said that, like some other parts of the ASB, the language of the prayers and declarations might be improved in terms of solemnity and imagery. Furthermore, the rites of ordination have an important *lex orandi, lex credendi* role in the Church. The modern pressures on the pastor, the increase in administration, and the diversity of parish and specialized ministries all tend to pull the pastor in many directions — some of which are not helpful. The prayers and declarations of the Ordinal call us all to order, they set goals for the Church, and challenge those in authority to enable the goals to become realities. They are a useful corrective against the tendency to mould the ministry into something akin to a modern management team. It is important to get the biblical ideas of ministry properly and imaginatively articulated in the liturgy.

One place where improvement is needed is in the rubrics for the setting of these rites. Ratcliff made a plea for the restoration of the ancient tradition that bishops should be consecrated on a Sunday in their own cathedrals amongst their own faithful, and this surely makes good pastoral sense. This principle ought to be extended to all ordinations of presbyters and deacons even if it entails many ordinations over a period of time. The bishop's presence secures the diocesan and catholic dimensions, but ordination in the parish church secures the practical *sitz im leben* of ministry.

The declaration and the ordination prayers should not only define each ministry, but also indicate their relationship to each other. Ratcliff suggested that in the ordination of presbyters, after the words 'work faithfully with all their fellow-servants [in Christ]' there should be included 'with their brethren in the ministry and with thy Chief Pastors, the Bishops'.[3] This he believed brought out the essentially 'collegiate' character of the relationship between bishops and presbyters, and the presbyters amongst themselves. Perhaps this needs to be included, though perhaps in less clumsy language than Ratcliff proposed. Furthermore, if there is now a permanent diaconate in the Church of England (and one hopes that ordination of women to the priesthood will not destroy this important recovered ministry) then this ministry needs a more distinctive profile. For far too long it has been overshadowed by the presbyterate, and deacons have been portrayed in the ordination rite as inferior ministers, and learner priests. This distinct ministry ought to be carefully stated in the rite. The ministry of deacons should not be identical to that of the presbyter apart from presiding at the Eucharist.

One point which might be considered is that in the declarations and ordination prayers, we might have examples of forms which could be common texts throughout the Anglican Communion, giving it some common identity.

Two other points need mentioning. First, insignia: Ratcliff argued against any insignia since this detracts from the ordination by prayer and the laying on of hands. However, secondary symbolism can be useful,[4] and Ratcliff conceded the use of the pastoral staff. However, the insignia should come immediately after the ordination prayer. It is questionable as to whether the Reformation 'porrection' of a Bible serves any useful purpose — it is surely more appropriate at baptism, since the word of God is entrusted to the whole Church, and the limitation of the New Testament to the diaconate suggests that there may be something 'Marcionite' about this Order! If the Bible is to be given at ordinations, then it should be given to all Orders. The chalice and paten are still quite appropriate insignia for presbyters, and a towel and bowl have good biblical and liturgical precedents to be utilized as diaconal *porrectio*. Although the ASB allows appropriate vesture, this surely detracts too much from the act of ordination itself, and is best left until the ordinands are actually engaged in liturgical celebrations in their parishes. The encouragement to concelebrate is dear to some Anglican hearts, but the present writer refused to concelebrate with the bishop at his own ordination!

Lastly, the part of the laity in ordination services needs to be reconsidered. They assent to the election of the candidate. The American and Canadian rites state that the Old Testament and Epistle readings should be read by layfolk. One wonders why a layperson should not read the declaration, for it is from the baptized that the deacons, presbyters and bishops are called out to the distinctive ministry. Some have suggested including 'parts' for representatives of other denominations — an ecumenical dimension. This surely should be resisted at all costs. Ordination in the Church of England is to the Anglican Communion, but also to the Church universal; any denominational 'part' suggests that ordination is more limited to the 'Anglican' ministry.

NOTES

1 For example, in the *Apostolic Tradition* of Hippolytus. See also *The Priesthood of the Ordained Ministry*, London, CBF, 1986.
2 Letter to Eric Kemp, 6 December 1965, p. 2 (Liturgical Commission Memorandum 168A).
3 Draft ordination Prayers prepared by E. C. Ratcliff, 5.1.1966 (Liturgical Commission Memorandum 168A).
4 Bryan D. Spinks, 'Symbolism in the Sacraments', in K. W. Stevenson, ed., *Symbolism and Liturgy* II, Grove Liturgical Study 26, Bramcote, Grove, 1981.

10

The Inauguration of Ministries

MARTIN DUDLEY

The anthropologist Meyer Fortes, writing about inauguration rituals, pointed to the 'mysterious quality of continuity through time . . . basic to the self-image of every society, modern, archaic, or primitive' which 'is in some way congealed in these installation ceremonies'.[1] Certainly the actions called institution or collation and induction are very ancient and the essential ritual actions are basically unchanged since feudal times. They operate in a multi-layered way and are resistant to change despite the fact that they originate in and represent a hierarchically ordered sacral society. Marc Bloch's description of feudal homage and fealty is, among other things, a description of the institution of a clerk to a benefice.[2] The multiplication of ministries has given rise to other forms of inauguration. They can usually be considered in terms of a modified service of institution. Institutions, installations and enthronements do express, and need to express continuity. With less traditional forms of ministry an act of inauguration might be more creatively expressive of what is involved. There can be no general prescription for those occasions.

The ecclesiastical law as presently constituted requires that the bishop should use his best endeavour to perform the institution in the parish church.[3] A necessary preamble, frequently incorporated in the ceremony, is the making of the oaths of allegiance to the sovereign and of canonical obedience to the bishop together with the Declaration of Assent, the latter being both an affirmation of faith and an undertaking to use only authorized forms of service 'in public prayer and administration of the sacraments'.[4] The institution is performed by the bishop reading the words of institution from a written instrument to which the episcopal seal is appended while the priest kneels before him and holds the seal. This recitation, with its operative words 'institute' or 'collate', 'invest' and 'commit', is the central and essential act. The instrument is then handed to the priest and the traditional words are said: 'Receive the cure of souls which is both yours and mine.' It is not clear that these words, said in Latin until quite recently, are now themselves essential, but they accompany and elucidate the act of handing the deed or document over, and are usually followed by the blessing of the minister.

Historically, there has been no general provision of a service of institution and it has been frequently done without any liturgical ceremony. Medieval canon law seems to assume that there will be a ceremony but does not require it or prescribe its shape. In the general liturgical revision of the last three decades, diocesan services have been written and rewritten so that they stress prevailing attitudes to ministry. In the process they have often become overburdened with parts written in for everyone and have obscured the basic structure and functions of the service. It may be worth stating what the service isn't. It isn't an occasion for a last farewell to an outgoing minister provided by coachloads of former parishioners. It isn't a reunion for the minister's family and old friends. It isn't a service in which every ornamental dignitary and office-holder, ecclesiastical and secular, diocesan, synodical, ecumenical and parochial, can have a walk-on part, much less a speaking one.

So what is it? What structures govern its form and content? Two can be immediately identified. First, and this is the aspect which seems to govern the thinking among bishops and their staff meetings, it is the delivery of a specific ministry to an individual by the appropriate canonical authority. The act of delivering this ministry makes explicit certain aspects of the nature of an episcopally and hierarchically ordered church. The minister is a person who stands in a specified relationship to the one who exercises authority, the bishop. Here the bishop is seen as the chief pastor within the diocese, to whom is committed the maintenance and teaching of the faith, the exercise of government, and the responsibility to ordain and send new ministers, to guide them and to enable them to fulfil their ministry. The minister is bound to the bishop in a common faith (as set out in the Declaration of Assent), by obedience and by a shared responsibility for the cure of souls. This relationship may not be very apparent at other times but in the act of transmitting authority it is made clear. It is expressed in the acts of institution and induction. The archdeacon, who has ordinary jurisdiction in certain matters, is in essence an agent of the bishop. He has a particular duty, as expressed in Canon C 22 (4) to ensure that those who hold ecclesiastical office perform their duties with diligence, and to 'bring to the bishop's attention what calls for correction or merits praise'. He inducts on the bishop's mandate.

Second, and this is the factor that is most important for the parish, it is the beginning of a new relationship between a minister and those for whom he or she cares, the community of faith in a place and its fringe. Although a rector or vicar has responsibility for a parish in a geographical sense, the 'people' so often mentioned in institution services who are invited to express a commitment to and with their new minister are in fact the 'faithful'. They are present as those who will be ministered to and as those who will share in ministering. Whilst this is not an appropriate occasion for a general renewal of baptismal promises or of commitment to mission, an expression of common purpose under Christ of bishop, minister, clergy and laity is surely desirable.

These more basic and obvious structures are complemented or confused by others, by those I have already proscribed, and by a desire to represent further areas of contact and ministry: the local community and its organizations, the deanery, and the ecumenical dimension. I think we must recognize that a single ritual action cannot carry the weight of all that is usually put upon it. The fundamental structures, expressing the relation of bishop and minister and faithful and minister, must be paramount. There is no reason why the institution of a new minister might not be succeeded in the days following by an ecumenical event, by a deanery event, replacing the perfunctory welcome from the rural dean made at chapter or synod, and by a social act in relation to the wider community, such as calling on the mayor or whatever else is appropriate. *Rites de passage* usually involve several ritual actions spread over time. The inauguration of a ministry should be treated as such a rite, and doing so involves little more than recognizing that the service of institution or licensing is one part, albeit the pivotal part, of the process of appointment and entering upon one's new ministry.

Before I offer some thoughts on how the service itself might be structured, I must answer the question of whether we need a generally authorized service contained in an official Church of England book or not. The prevailing situation of diocesan services seems to (a) suit the bishops, (b) appal the clergy, and (c) keep diocesan liturgical committees busy. Most of the services now in use, in my limited experience, are fairly conservative, and while there is remarkable diversity between dioceses, there isn't within dioceses. Bishops, archdeacons and registrars like them simple, straightforward and unchanging. This is fully understandable when you think of the stress involved in adjusting to a constant stream of improvised services. Directory-style proposals from diocesan committees have in consequence generally been rejected. In some dioceses institutions are never eucharistic and in others they always are, the new minister assisting the bishop or concelebrating with him. The style is usually set by the diocesan bishop. I think it unlikely, therefore, that a single new service or directory-style proposals would meet with general episcopal approval. However, it would be worth producing three or four services to meet the needs of particular forms of inauguration that could be offered as types on which diocesan services could be based. Like the *Lent, Holy Week, Easter* services they could be authorized by the bishop in their original or diocesan forms, or not at all, but they would at least provide a standard and a resource.

The form of the service should be determined by the underlying structures. In institutions and inductions the relation to the bishop and to the parish needs to be clearly expressed. The former is expressed in the legal preambles (which could be done privately but are better done as a public affirmation), the act of institution by the bishop, and of induction by the archdeacon. The latter has no obvious shape, but has taken that of questions and answers about those aspects of ministry represented in the church building by the font, lectern, pulpit and altar. A portion of Scripture is usually read, some aspect of ministry specifically cited and a question is put to the new minister and/or the people. Here is an example of 'Commitment to Mission' at the church door:[5]

The Rural Dean reads Luke 4:16–19: 'The Spirit of the Lord is upon me . . .'

The Bishop: It is our joyful task to bring Christ's Gospel to all people. Are you willing, by word and deed, to proclaim that Gospel?

Minister: The Gospel of Christ is my joy. I am resolved, to

the best of my ability, to proclaim that Gospel by word and by deed, bringing Christ's message of grace in all areas of life.

Congregation: We share in the joy of the Gospel. As we work together we will proclaim that Gospel to the best of our ability, in whichever situation we find ourselves. So help us, God. Amen.

More recently, as evidenced in the American Episcopal Prayer Book, signs of various sorts have been used, sometimes added to the question-and-answer routine.[6]

. . . accept this water, and help the bishop baptize in obedience to our Lord.

. . . receive this stole, and be among us as pastor and priest.

. . . use this oil, and be among us as healer and reconciler.

. . . take this bread and wine, and be among us to break the Bread and bless the Cup.

Both approaches raise questions, the former about the use of the Bible and the latter about signs and symbols. On the whole we now, rightly, eschew the multiple use of detached biblical passages, especially if their sense is manipulated to suit specific purposes. Signs must also be employed sparingly and handled with caution. Their use can easily become absurd — 'receive these ashes, and be among us as one who buries the dead'! It can also obscure the central ritual act, just as the presentation of chalice and paten, the *traditio instrumentorum*, obscured the laying on of hands with prayer at ordination in the Middle Ages.

The basic pattern I want to suggest is this:

Preparation Greeting
Introduction to the Service
(Rite of Penance)
Collect

Ministry of the Word
Readings
Sermon
Hymn invoking the Holy Spirit
Litany (as at ordinations in ASB with an appropriate alternative paragraph for an Institution)

Institution or Licensing
Presentation of Minister
Declarations
Affirmation of Ministry at font, pulpit and/or chancel step, and altar
Act of Institution

Induction

The Welcome
(if a Eucharist, the Peace)

Either the Eucharist continues or, if the service is non-eucharistic, it may conclude with an act of celebration of new ministry (such as that used in the Diocese of Lincoln).

It should be clear throughout that the bishop is presiding and he, rather than the archdeacon, rural dean, or, worse, the deanery synod lay chairman, should ask the questions during the affirmations. Those affirmations should concern the proclamation of the gospel and admission of new members to the Church (font), study and exposition of Scripture and preaching (pulpit), marriage, penance, visiting the sick, burial of the dead, etc. (chancel step), and the Eucharist (altar). They conclude with the act of institution in front of the altar. If the use of signs is desired, they could be incorporated into the Welcome, with first representatives of the parish, and then of deanery, diocese, ecumenical bodies, and the local community being involved. There should be a lighter touch to this, precisely because the most appropriate sign might be something apparently trivial. Signs of ministry might be presented by the parish, a list of dates of meetings by the synod chairman, with a strong encouragement to be present and to play a part, a Bible by an ecumenical representative expressing a common faith, and so on. The mayor, for example, could present a map of the area, saying:

> Welcome to our town. We give you this map of it, and hope that we will see you often in its streets, and that you will play a full part in its life.

One final point of concern is the presence of other clergy, usually called 'visiting clergy'. They may be divided into three categories: those who are in the congregation, the robed clergy who are visitors, and diocesan/deanery clergy. If the minister is new to the diocese, then he is joining the *presbyterium*, the body of priests gathered around the bishop and, in particular, joining the clergy of the deanery. In a heavily ritualized action such as this the clergy are not ornamental. Their presence has significance and should not be minimized. The clergy of the diocese should not be seated in some out of the way place and the deanery clergy might well process in with the rural dean. Entry processions of clergy who robed in the vicarage or church hall are notoriously difficult to marshal but the order should not be random or haphazard. Robed lay ministers should come first; then the deacons; then the priests, with the 'visiting clergy' differentiated from those of the diocese among whom the new minister will have his place.

An institution expresses only one aspect of the life of the

Church. To say that it makes little of the role of the laity or of the relations implied in synodical government or of being Churches together in the confession of a common faith is to make a reasonable observation. It is not intended to express any of those things as its major theme. It speaks of ordained ministry, of the duty and office involved in it, of how necessary orders are in the Church of Christ, and of how people ought to esteem their ministers in their office. In this way it is in complete continuity through time with the meaning of that ministry found in the Ordinal of the Book of Common Prayer. When few parishioners are present with any frequency or regularity at ordinations, the opportunity that an institution offers is not to be spurned or minimized.

There will be pastoral and liturgical ministries that begin without the presence of a bishop, those of assistant curates, parish deacons, licensed readers, and of those licensed to assist in administering the holy communion. The basic principles evidenced in institutions apply also here. That is to say, an act of inauguration should clearly indicate the structures and relations involved in the ministry. From ordinations we also get the principle that those admitted to any office should then be allowed to exercise it. When an assistant curate is a priest, then he will, of course, preside at the Eucharist, and the specifically inaugural acts will of necessity be limited to welcomings and the use of signs and symbols, unless a parish opts to have some declaration made which stresses, as the institution does, the bonds linking the incumbent and the curate. This would involve statements of faith, respect for authority, and unity in pastoral ministry. In basic form this could derive from the Declaration of Assent. The same procedure would be followed for a deacon, though inaugural actions can be more easily achieved whilst the ministry of deacons is unfamiliar in many parishes. Presentations could express the range of ministry involved: a stole for liturgy, an educational book for teaching and study, a cake to express the social dimensions. These do not need words and the full meaning for the people may come from *who* makes the presentation rather than from *what* is presented. Biblical concepts of ministry might suggest other ritual possibilities which stress service. Accepting the cautions offered by Perham and Stevenson on the washing of feet, a parish priest might still appropriately wash the feet of his deacon or curate as they begin their ministry. This act might be accompanied by the words based on the Canadian rite for Maundy Thursday:

> My brother [or sister], on the night before his death Jesus set an example for disciples by washing their feet, an act of humble service. He taught that strength and growth in the life of the kingdom of God come not by power, authority, or even miracle, but by such lowly service. Called to ministry together in this place, I now wash your feet that I may recall whose servant I am by following the example of my Master. In doing this I remind you that what I do for you is also to be done by you to others, for 'a servant is not greater than his master, nor is one who is sent greater than the one who sent him. If you know these things, blessed are you if you do them.'[7]

The beginning of the ministry of a reader needs to be carefully handled precisely because, in cassock, surplice and scarf, readers look so clerical. Those who have received permission to assist with the distribution of communion might be installed with a simple rite in which, after words of explanation from the president, they affirm their willingness to serve and receive their letter of authorization. They might then administer communion *in both kinds* while the president, on this occasion, having given them communion, returns to his seat.

It must be stressed again that inauguration rituals can extend over time. Those that are performed at the main parish

Eucharist may not be seen by at least some of the people who will be affected by a new ministry. The most effective form of inauguration at the mid-week Eucharist, at the school or old people's home, might be nothing more than a formal introduction, brief words of welcome and some applause. Parishes must be sensitive to the need for a new minister to find his or her place and a series of acts, all of them brief and simple, can aid this process.

NOTES

1   E. Fortes, 'Of Installation Ceremonies', *Proceedings of the Royal Anthropological Institute for 1967* (London 1968), pp. 5–20; cited by Janet L. Nelson, *Politics and Ritual in Early Medieval Europe* (London, Hambledon Press, 1986), p. 283.
2   Marc Bloch, *Feudal Society* (London, Routledge & Kegan Paul, 1965), vol. 1, pp. 145ff.
3   Canons of the Church of England, Canon 10 (5).
4   Canons 13, 14 and 15.
5   Diocese of Gloucester, *Service of Institution and Induction*, 1989.
6   *Book of Common Prayer* (of the American Episcopal Church), pp. 561–2.
7   *The Book of Alternative Services of the Anglican Church of Canada*, p. 305.

11

Worship and Evangelism

BRYAN SPINKS

One of the more popular rationales heard in the 1960s and 1970s to justify the revision of the Prayer Book, and the production of the ASB, was that the old forms of liturgy were no longer understood properly by many people, and were barriers to spiritual growth; furthermore, they no longer drew people to church. There was — quite rightly — no suggestion that God did not like the old forms, but they were no longer comprehensible and inspiring to many worshippers. One concern of the ASB was, therefore, to recapture a principle dear to Cranmer, that liturgy should be understood by the people, because it should serve for edification of the Body of Christ — hence the modern direct style of language in much of the ASB. Some clergy (rather naive, and rarely themselves directly engaged in the process of liturgical revision) even suggested that the new services would attract folk back into the growing rows of empty pews. Yet we do well to ask just how far these dual expectations of liturgy — edification and evangelism — are at all justified.

According to the Reformed theologian J. J. von Allmen, worship is not *per se* addressed to outsiders, and neither is it even specifically directed to the Church.[1] Worship summons the Church together, making it visible. But it is the *Church*, the *qahal*, the baptized community which is summoned. Its worship is a highly cultic activity, and its object, as of all true doxology, is God. If we may change the imagery, in worship the nuptial community speaks in intimate language with the bridegroom. The language of intimate lovers has its own secret vocabulary, its own special code; it, together with the acts of love-making, are not primarily to entertain the neighbours or peeping Toms. It ought to be conceded that worship is not primarily an evangelistic exercise, and should not be made a substitute for evangelism.

However, von Allmen (rather grudgingly perhaps) admits that although primarily addressed to God (*systole*), worship is nevertheless by its very nature indirectly addressed to the world (*diastole*).[2] Indeed, von Allmen may have underestimated the impact of what he terms *diastole*. Wesley, it will be recalled, described the Eucharist as a 'converting ordinance', and he was speaking from experience, not from a handbook on liturgical theology. The language of lovers serves to excite the lovers themselves, and to intensify and deepen their love for one another; it has also been known to be quite a turn-on for those who inadvertently, or deliberately, eavesdrop! Liturgy can have an evangelistic by-product in two senses: liturgical formation (or edification) of the worshippers; and a converting power (or outreach).

How far is the ASB successful in these? First, in terms of liturgical formation, the services themselves have proved reasonably popular and have undoubtedly resulted in a greater theological awareness amongst worshippers, a greater sense of belonging to a community, and many of the prayers have helped the devotional life of the Church. No longer is the odd doctrine of royal supremacy promoted through prayer, and God's providence is put in better perspective. Yet in so far as the criticism of the style of much of the ASB language is valid, the Christian community is starved of evocative imagery; it is often too didactic and wooden, and in places too much like the *Daily Telegraph*. Like Richard Baxter, the ASB expects the mind to inform the heart; we need the touch of Jeremy Taylor to remind us that the heart can sometimes surprise the mind! Love-making needs variety and romance unless it is to become a dull routine. The revision of 2000 needs to consider this aspect carefully.

What of outreach? In many ways the proliferation of 'Family Services' is a judgement upon both the Prayer Book and the ASB. The former is too quaint and archaic for many, and seems to appeal to those with refined literary taste. The ASB on the other hand, quite apart from the charge of being 'middle-class', has with some justification been described as 'exclusive'. In heightening the consciousness of the Church as being the Body of Christ, it has made a great chasm between those within and those outside. Examples are given of the 'folk-religion' people who arrive for weddings and funerals, and now less often for baptisms, and who are unable to join in the Lord's Prayer which they learnt as a child. Or the demise of Matins and the proliferation of the Parish Communion, where there is a message of 'We are the Body of Christ and communicate; you aren't and can't'. The 'Family Service' has tended to be an *ad hoc* emendation of Matins, or an *ex nihilo* creation (often turning order into chaos and darkness) to provide a bridge between the outsiders and the more self-conscious cultic community. These services are more consciously evangelistic in using simpler language and forms, with modern music, choruses and guitars. The material has frequently been thematic to drive home the message. The problem here is that many of these services are banal and childish to the point of insult to worshipper and Almighty God. Frequently the whole event has more of the air of the classroom than a celebration; or to return to the nuptial imagery, more like a lecture on sex techniques than an act of love-making. The service fails to worship God. Also many fail in their rationale. Too many people seem content to attend the bridge services, and are content to remain on the bridge. They

103

don't want to cross over to the main diet of worship. They are happier listening to talk of love-making, but don't want to make love themselves!

And yet there is a need for such services. There are folk who are shy of clergy visits (an event which has already died out in some parishes!) and who like to approach God on their own terms and in their own time by attending worship — either because the children are involved, or the banns are being read, or someone has died, or there is a crisis, or simply out of plain curiosity in the divine. God moves in mysterious ways. Liturgy cannot always at every point cater for all these eventualities, but there should be provision for people to 'bring their humanity to God', and to encounter God.[3]

The recent GS 898 *Patterns for Worship* produced by the Liturgical Commission is, it is to be hoped, a step in the direction of eliminating the more banal worship, and providing 'graded' material which can act as a bridge, but with language which is powerful enough to convert. Use alone will determine just what, if any, of this material succeeds in this area. The revision of 2000 may be less permissive than *Patterns*, but will surely carry some of its forms and guidelines. It will make it clear that Anglican worship has a structure, and forms should be used which echo or overlap with the more usual or traditional diet of worship — creeds, collects, responses, prayers of thanksgiving, etc. And these services need to be carefully worked out to link with or lead people to baptism, confirmation (however this might be conceived in 2000) and full eucharistic participation. Potentially the *qahal* is open to all; the world is not only invited to the wedding, but to be the Bride. Liturgy needs to be powerful enough to allow the worshippers to grow in love — even fall in love — with the Bridegroom, and to make love.

NOTES

1 J. J. von Allmen, *Worship: Its Theology and Practice* (London 1965), p. 77.
2 ibid.
3 See my essay, 'The Liturgical Ministry of the Laity', in T. J. Talley, ed., *A Kingdom of Priests: Liturgical Formation of the People of God*, Alcuin/Grove Liturgical Study 5 (Bramcote, Grove, 1988), pp. 20–7.

Postscript:
Investing in Liturgy
for the New Century

BRYAN SPINKS

In his recent book on the background to the compilation of the ASB, Ronald Jasper notes the general interest shown in liturgical revision in the Church of England. But he adds:

> However, healthy widespread interest must be based on solid foundations. Activities such as expert training in the leading of public worship or cross-fertilization with other disciplines require in the first instance study at the highest level. Here, sadly, the Churches in this country are at a disadvantage. Few universities bother to include liturgy as a major element in their theological studies and many ignore it altogether. Any kind of Liturgical Institute with a full-time staff of scholars just does not exist. Dom Gregory Dix commented some fifty years ago that liturgy was trapped in a kind of whirlpool, with too few scholars chasing too few books around and around in a vicious never-ending circle. That situation still exists today.[1]

For all the faults of the ASB, real or otherwise, the fact is that the Church of England can think itself fortunate that it was able to produce a work of such quality at all. It was fortunate indeed that it did have scholars such as Ratcliff, Couratin and

Willis, and then Jasper, Cuming, Buchanan and Whitaker —
fortunate because as Ronald Jasper notes, competent liturgical
revision needs some degree of expert training, but England has
poor provisions for training such people. Liturgy is also given a
low status. For example, Ronald Jasper was Reader in Liturgy
at King's College, London — already a step down from its
status as a professorial chair when held by Ratcliff. On Jasper's
retirement from the Readership, the post became a part-time
lectureship held by Geoffrey Cuming in conjunction with a
similar part-time post at Ripon College, Cuddesdon. On
Cuming's retirement it was absorbed by church historians.
Similar depressing tales can be told of the subject's fate
elsewhere. At present no English university has a full-time
post in liturgics, and where it is offered as a subject within
theology, it is taught by people who actually hold other
appointments. This situation, which is not new, has had a
knock-on effect in Theological Colleges, which have found it
difficult to find liturgy tutors, and the subject is rarely taught
by someone who holds a post-graduate degree in the discipline.
Inevitably, the standard of the training of the clergy in this
area is low. The cut-backs in education have exacerbated an
already poor situation, since there are fewer opportunities for
post-graduate work in theology at all. Changes in methods of
training in Theological Colleges have also removed the older
possibility of an MA or MPhil as part of training. The recent
remarks by the Prince of Wales about the language of the ASB
may not have been entirely fair, but there are few Stella
Brooks or David Frosts, and the Church on the one hand
slates the language produced by Liturgical Commissions, but
seems to lack the will to bring together literature experts and
liturgists. Ronald Jasper's book betrays the fact that, behind
the politics, the ASB was a frustrating part-time production,
on a shoe-string budget of time and money.

At a meeting at Lambeth Palace in November 1985 a group

of liturgists was invited to discuss with the Archbishop the serious state of liturgical scholarship in this country, covering the university situation, liturgical formation, and the possibility of an Institute for Liturgy. The eventual outcome has been a contribution of £10,000 towards a tenured appointment of Chaplain/Research Fellow in Liturgy (the Cuming Fellow) at St Chad's College, Durham. This is certainly a step in the right direction, but on its own will be negligible. A delegation from the present Liturgical Commission visited the Irish Institute of Pastoral Liturgy, Carlow, in November 1987, and made certain suggestions for strengthening liturgical study in the Church of England and in England generally. So far its suggestions have not been acted upon.

The Church of England lays great emphasis on the liturgy as a source of doctrine and teaching, as well as of edification and as an aid in spiritual development. There is, therefore, both a serious theological and aesthetic side to liturgical composition. If the Liturgy of 2000 — and beyond — is to be worthy of the name 'Liturgy', then some sound investment — financial and otherwise — ought to be made now to ensure a continuing stream of scholars and liturgically aware pastors to develop our liturgical tradition. A whole series of measures needs to be taken:

(1) Liturgy needs to be restored in selected university faculties (or safeguarded where it now survives), and programmes for undergraduates and post-graduates developed. Different universities might offer different specialisms: liturgy and history, liturgy and dogmatics, liturgy and literature, liturgy and music. The state is unlikely to fund such posts; it would be for the Church to raise the money, investing in its own future.

(2) Theological Colleges — especially those situated near universities — ought to encourage their liturgy tutors to

complete post-graduate degrees in liturgy, and each Theological College should offer a one-year or three-year bursary for post-graduate liturgical research.

(3) Use could be made of the Irish Institute, allowing it to become more ecumenical in its outlook. Anglican Theological College students and parish priests on study leave could be encouraged to spend time in study there.

(4) The Liturgical Commission needs full-time staff, both to do academic research and field work (if necessary, combined with university posts). Compared with the Board of Education, for example, liturgy appears to be a low priority. If worship is important (and whatever else the Church does, it engages in worship) then it should be seen to be important.

(5) A programme of liturgical formation should be worked out in the dioceses, with a full-time senior appointment; the person will be a residentiary Canon (cf. Director of Diocesan Education) — as was suggested to the Bishop of St Albans by the retiring Chairman of the Diocesan Liturgical Committee, John Mullett. Diocesan Liturgical Committees need to be fully involved in in-service training of the clergy, and in lay education.

Urgent action is needed on these points if the revision of 2000 and future revision are to be good liturgy. 'For to him who has will more be given; and from him who has not, even what he has will be taken away.'

NOTE

1 R. C. D. Jasper, *The Development of the Anglican Liturgy 1662–1980* (London, SPCK, 1989), p. 364.